GREGORY
BE HAPPY!

SHTICK SHIFT

SHTICK SHIFT

Jewish Humor in the 21st Century

SIMCHA WEINSTEIN

Fort Lee, New Jersey

Published by Barricade Books Inc.
185 Bridge Plaza North
Suite 308-A
Fort Lee, NJ 07024
www.barricadebooks.com

Library of Congress Cataloging-in-Publication Data
A copy of this title's Library of Congress Cataloging-in-Publication Data is available on request from the Library of Congress.

ISBN 13: 978-1-56980-352-3

10 9 8 7 6 5 4 3 2 1

Manufactured in the United States of America

CONTENTS

ACKNOWLEDGMENTS   9

PREFACE: Put on Your *Yarmulke*   11

INTRODUCTION:
Something From Nothing: Jewish
Comedy in a New Century   17

ONE: Jew Gold: Self-Fulfilling Stereotypes and
Unfulfilling Wealth   35

TWO: Raising the Bar: Bling Mitzvah   51

THREE: Beyond Bubbe: The 21st-Century
Jewish Family   63

FOUR: Fake News, Real Impact   79

FIVE: Seriously Funny: Anti-Semitism
and Self-Hatred   93

CONCLUSION:
Cool, Jew?   111

GLOSSARY   119

END NOTES   123

This book is dedicated to my father, Eddie Weinstein, the personification of the word mensch, who raised me on a rich diet of nurturing love and classic British comedy.

ACKNOWLEDGMENTS

Thanks to...

Steven Bergson, Davida Breier, Vincent Brook, Benyamin Cohen, Samuel Freedman, Rama Hughes, Lisa Alcalay Klug, Gersh Kuntzman, Mark Pinsky, Stephen and Sydnie Salmieri, Rivka Slonim, Saul Sudin and Joley Wood: Your honest kvetching made this a better book.

Carole Stuart, Sharon Berger and Ivy McFadden: The kind and courageous team at Barricade Books.

Blanca Madani: Who I forgot to thank in my last book, so I'm doing it here instead!

George and Pamela Rohr: Thank you for your support and belief in all my antics.

Rabbi Aaron and Shternie Raskin: Wise mentors to my wife and I. It is a privilege to work under these incomparable Chabad-Lubavitch emissaries.

The congregation of B'nai Avraham: I am inspired by

your wholly (and holy) unorthodox approach to Ortho-dox Judaism.

Rabbis DovBer Pinson, Moshe Hubner, Menachem Schmidt and Shimon Apisdorf: Great sages with great senses of humor.

Kathy Shaidle, my editor: "Five feet of fury" indeed!

Stewart Shimberg, my trusted webmaster: We could not be farther apart ideologically—or closer in friendship.

To all the students at the Downtown Brooklyn Jewish Student Foundation and especially those at the Pratt Institute: This book is the culmination of many conversations over literally gallons of chicken soup (although, thanks to Pratt veggies, it has now grudgingly become asparagus soup). This book is as much yours as it is mine.

My dear friends and family on the other side of the pond in Manchester, England, who continue to be there for me—even with an ever-growing beard.

To my brother David and his lovely new wife Naomi, parents and parents-in-law and nanny: Unconditional love rocks!

Mendel and Eli: Daddy has given up hoping the two of you will ever sleep through the night. My forced insomnia has given me time to write books, so I guess a thank-you is in order.

Ariella: I'm in awe of your grace, humility and wisdom. Thanks for teaching me timeless truths as opposed to the twenty-first-century's cynical "truthiness."

PREFACE

PUT ON YOUR *YARMULKE*

"The goyim don't know how to laugh,
they haven't suffered enough."[1]
—*Paul Mazursky*

Growing up Jewish in cold, rainy Manchester, England, I always knew that I was "a little different." My parents promised me a post-bar mitzvah growth spurt. (I'm still waiting.) And when the No. 135 bus took me home each day and stopped to pick up the kids from the local Catholic school, I'd shove my *yarmulke* even deeper into my pocket. Getting picked on by the big kids for being short and shy was bad enough. Getting picked on for being Jewish was much worse. But there was no point provoking the local anti-Semites by exhibiting my religiosity. These bullies weren't the majority, by any means—but that didn't make them any less scary.

My fears at the bus stop followed me into Hebrew school, where I learned all about centuries of Jewish suffering and oppression. When I walked back outside, our synagogue had been spray-painted, yet again, with (misspelled) obscenities.

Like many Jewish families, the standing joke at our family's Passover seder table was, "They tried to kill us, we survived, let's eat." But it didn't seem all that funny to me, not when the tombstones in the local Jewish cemetery were defaced with swastikas. And so, like many underdogs, I sought solace in popular culture and the world of superheroes. (In case anybody wants to learn more, I've divulged my affection for caped crusaders in my book *Up, Up and Oy Vey!: How Jewish History, Culture and Values Shaped the Comic Book Superhero.*) Within that alternative universe of "Zap! Pow! Bam!," *nebbishy* nerds like Clark Kent beat up the bad guys, not the other way around.

Halfway through high school, however, I made a life-changing discovery. Beneath my nebbishy exterior, I possessed a hidden "super power" of my own: the power of humor. Suddenly, I became the class clown, cracking up my teachers and classmates. Now that the cool kids liked me more, the mean ones were less prone to beat me up. I learned later that I was in good company—many famous Jewish comedians had been class clowns, too.

At the time, however, I knew almost nothing about the tremendous impact Jews have had on comedic history. Instead, I'd subconsciously tapped into this long, storied tradition. Like countless Jews before and since, I discovered that suffering inspires humor, which in turn can be used to fight oppression.

Only later did I take that *yarmulke* out of my pocket. I'd studied film at university, and after graduation I began a rewarding career in movie and television production. But something was missing. After all, the entertainment industry revolves around all things superficial and trendy. As I looked for something more serious to which I could dedicate my life, I found myself thinking more and more about my faith.

I started taking classes, and became more observant. My spiritual awakening was nothing dramatic—unless swapping movie sets for "rabbi school" (yeshiva) counts as "dramatic." During that journey, I met rabbis and rebbetzins who became my new mentors and "super heroes." The men were full of wit and wonder, nothing like the stuffy "white shirt/black suit" penguins I'd expected. The women surprised me, too. They were outrageous, confident and free-thinking, not stereotypical, shmatteh-wearing submissive kitchen slaves. Through these holy Hebrew jesters, I finally came to appreciate those dark-humored jokes around the seder table, and the very real role comedy has played in helping Jews survive centuries of persecution.

Indeed, humor—which is all about paradox and a sense of the absurd—plays a significant role in the Jewish faith. As the old joke goes: If you don't think God has a sense of humor, you haven't seen a platypus.

Or better yet, consider the festival of Purim, inspired by the biblical Book of Esther. Purim celebrates the time that the Jews of ancient Persia were saved from genocide. Okay, so that may not sound like a recipe for hilarity, but that's exactly what makes the story a great taproot of Jewish humor. The tale relies on split-second reversals of fortune—called hippuch in Hebrew. The only difference between tragedy and comedy is the way the story ends, and the Purim story certainly wraps up with an amusing punch line. Haman, the chief advisor to the Persian king Achashverosh, secretly plots to kill all the

Jews in the kingdom. Disaster seems inevitable. Little does he know that the king's wife, Queen Esther, is Jewish herself. Ooops! In an ironic twist, Haman ends up executed on the very gallows he built to hang the Jews. To this day, Jews commemorate this victorious reversal of fortune with a *purimshpil* (which means a "Purim game" in Yiddish), dressing up in costumes inspired by the Bible story, and perpetuating the tradition of linking the bitter with the sweet, and tragedy with comedy.

These lighthearted Purim activities serve a serious purpose: to remind us that persecution still exists and shows no sign of abating. On New Year's Eve, 1999, the world pinned its hopes on the dawn of the new millennium, when we would finally bid farewell to the bloodiest century in history. Instead, the twenty-first century ushered in the new Intifada, the 9/11 terrorist attacks and other deadly bombings in London and Madrid. And who would have dared imagine that the ancient and barbaric practice of beheading would reenter the modern world with the execution of Jewish "infidels" like *Wall Street Journal* reporter Daniel Pearl? Nations like Iran and North Korea pose threats to world peace, while reports of genocide in Darfur seem to indicate we have failed to learn the lessons of the Holocaust. Closer to home, the evening news presents a nightmare vision of violence, economic meltdown and pointless tragedy, coupled with reports of shallow, shameless celebrity insanity.

Despite these dark turns in the annals of history, the United States generally remains a safe haven for the Jewish people. But, ironically, America's embrace of the

Jewish people has a shadow side: rampant assimilation and secularism that threatens the future of our faith.

Sadly, I witnessed something I never expected: the same hatred I saw as a child in England, here in my adopted home of New York City. In the autumn of 2007, our local synagogue was vandalized, along with another synagogue on our block. The culprits spray-painted and scratched more than twenty swastikas onto cars, and stuffed handwritten flyers reading "Israel: Land of Pigs" and "All Jews Die" on windshields. And this was in Brooklyn Heights, a leafy, gentrified neighborhood. Coincidentally (or not) the vandalism occurred just a few hours after anti-Semitic Iranian President Mahmoud Ahmadinejad spewed his rhetoric not far away, at Columbia University.

Thankfully, diligent police work paid off and a few months later, a suspect was indicted on almost one hundred counts of criminal mischief and other charges. An arsenal of weapons, including pipe bombs and firearms, was uncovered in his apartment. Our community was relieved, but also disturbed by the news that the suspect was a local man—who claimed to be Jewish. His home was just a short distance from my office; I've probably passed him on the sidewalk many times.

What a chilling reminder of the very real dangers we face today.

With all the *tzurus* in the world, we might well ask: What is there for twenty-first-century Jewish comedians to joke about?

The surprising answer—plenty.

Luckily for us all, a veritable army of next-generation Jewish comedians are now on the scene, ready to slay the world's modern-day Hamans with their wit.

But before we meet these new Jewish jokers, let's pay tribute to the funny men and women who paved their way.

INTRODUCTION

SOMETHING FROM NOTHING: JEWISH COMEDY IN A NEW CENTURY

"It's [Jewish humor] less polite, less European, and more—
well, American. And if Jews are becoming less Jewish, in
some cases that may be balanced by the fact that America
seems to be getting more Jewish."[1]
—*William Novak and Moshe Waldoks,*
The Big Book of Jewish Humor *(25th Anniversary Edition)*

Today's Jewish world would be unrecognizable to our *bubbes* and *zaydes*. Hollywood hipsters on spiritual safari now happily hand over big bucks to study (inauthentic) *Kabbalah*, the same ancient Jewish texts you couldn't pay me to read when I was a kid. (I preferred comic books, remember?) In 2003, *Time Out New York* announced the arrival of "the New Super Jews."[2] These "edgy young taste-makers" were busy "forging a hip new Jewish identity" in the entertainment industry. Fast-forward just a few years, and *Billboard*'s Best Reggae Artist of 2006 is a black-hat Hassid called Matisyahu, while the hottest comedic talent is a guy named Sacha Baron Cohen (better known for his high-five Kazakh alter-ego, Borat).

As a rabbi for one of America's most prestigious art schools, the Pratt Institute in New York City, I work with college students every day. From the countless examples that cross my desk, I can say without a doubt that it has never before been so hip to be Jewish. It would seem that in the twenty-first century, being Jewish is, by definition, cool.

What's more, a 2005 study by the National Foundation for Jewish Culture revealed that while many Jews in their twenties and thirties were not affiliated with traditional institutions such as synagogues and Jewish community centers, they were nevertheless deeply engaged in Jewish culture. This generation's Jewishness is more offbeat and cultural than mainstream religious. It manifests itself in cheeky T-shirt slogans like "Jewcy" and "What would Maimonides do?" It is celebrated with readings of the Purim *megillah* in nightclubs, accompanied by tequila shots. In that cultural study, authors Steven Cohen and Ari Kelman note: "The non-Jewish venues, such as Joe's Pub, The Slipper Room or The Knitting Factory, provide considerable cultural cachet, generational comfort, low entrance barriers, and no expectations for future obligations, all important criteria for this generation when choosing leisure-time activities."[3]

Irreverent humor with an "in your *punim*" attitude is now the *lingua franca* of young Jewish adults, whose common reference points come from *The Simpsons*, not the synagogue.

It hasn't always been this way.

Sure, everyone knows that Jewish comedians dominated the American humor scene throughout much of the twentieth century. But their forerunners, the two million Jewish immigrants who pioneered communal

Jewish life in the United States between 1880 and 1924 were the ones who brought a very specific brand of humor to their new land: the sly, verbally ingenious situational comedy of the *shtetl*, with its stock comic characters: the *schnorrer* (cheapskate), the *nudnik* (pest) and the *gonif* (thief).

To get an idea of the difference a century of assimilation and acceptance can make, compare early Jewish vaudeville star Fanny Brice to Comedy Central's Sarah Silverman. Brice made quaint tunes like "Second Hand Rose" and "My Man" famous, whereas Silverman's notorious musical compositions include her paean to the elderly, "You're Gonna Die Soon," and the infamous "I Love You More (Than Jews Love Money)."

Early Jewish humor on the American stage, like Brice's exaggerated, put-on Yiddish accent, retained its unique "old-country" flavor even as immigrants found some security and success in the New World. With a massive audience in New York City, local Yiddish theater not only flourished during the 1910s and 1920s, it also served as a launching pad for performers who made the move first to mainstream vaudeville and then to big time showbiz beyond the confines of Manhattan. At the same time, the Marx Brothers, the Ritz Brothers and the Three Stooges brought their winning vaudeville routines to the silver screen. Jack Benny enjoyed enormous success in radio. (So did one very unlikely star: Edgar Bergen. Perhaps today, better known as the father of actress Candice—best known for her starring role in the sitcom *Murphy Brown*—Edgar Bergen was a ventriloquist. A ventriloquist on the radio? Hey, these were simpler times.)

While some of their routines might have been a little subversive, none of these performers presented a threat to American middle-class sensibilities. They never came right out and said, "Look, everybody! I'm Jewish!" And for good reason.

Often barred from joining "restricted" country clubs or staying at mainstream hotels, American Jews created their own. They began establishing their own resorts in upstate New York in the 1940s. There were so many of them that the area soon became known as the Borscht Belt. This string of holiday camps and hotels in the Catskills gave generations of Jewish performers an opportunity to develop what would become a distinctive performing style. A typical Catskills joke is corny, clean (by today's standards, anyway) and has an unmistakable "two-part" rhythm:

> The doctor gave a man six months to live. The man couldn't pay his bill, so the doctor gave him another six months.

> A car hit an elderly Jewish man. The doctor says, "Are you comfortable?" The man says, "I make a good living."

Eventually, this unique *cholent* of jokes, mockery and song and dance became synonymous with the genre now known as stand-up comedy. Take one self-deprecating, slightly desperate persona in a cheap tux, add a hostile, rapid-fire delivery that belies that *nebbishy* exterior, and you've got the classic Borscht Belt comic, a figure who gives the phrase "passive-aggressive" a new meaning.

The performers who honed their craft in the Catskills are legend. So are their aliases. The cast includes Mel Brooks (born Melvin Kaminsky), Joan Rivers (born Joan Molinsky), Danny Kaye (born David Daniel Kaminsky), George Burns (born Nathan Birnbaum), Rodney Dangerfield (born Jacob Cohen), Woody Allen (born Allen Stewart Konigsberg) and Milton Berle (born Mendel Berlinger), to name only a few. Speaking of "names," note how many of these comics "Americanized" their stage names, removing Mosaic overtones to sound more showbiz. In more recent years, this practice has become less widespread—just think of Sarah Silverman and Sacha Baron Cohen.

Two modern inventions led to the decline of the Borscht Belt (today familiar to most young people, Jews and non-Jews alike, only as the setting for the beloved 1987 romance film *Dirty Dancing*). First, the invention of affordable air-conditioning made New York City summers more bearable, and trips to the cooler Catskills unnecessary. More importantly, those new-fangled television sets became even more popular than air conditioners. The networks needed talent, and plenty of it, to fill up all those broadcasting hours, and with their wide appeal and proven successes, Jewish comics fit the bill. As the 1950s progressed, the cathode ray tube became the new Catskills.

This epoch-making evolutionary shift can be summed up in one example: Sid Caesar's *Your Show of Shows* (1950–1954), not only the inspiration for *Saturday Night Live*, but also almost every other sketch show in the history of American television. Of the program's eleven writers, ten were Jewish. Borscht Belt veterans like Mel Brooks collaborated with soon-to-be famous names like Neil Simon, Carl Reiner, a teenaged Woody Allen, and Larry Gelbart, who went on to create *M*A*S*H*. Years later, the legendary *Your Show of Shows* was fondly remembered with nostalgic cinematic valentines like the hit film *My Favorite Year* (1982) and Neil Simon's autobiographical Broadway play, *Laughter on the 23rd Floor* (1993).

The exotic charm of the occasional Yiddish word found its way into *Your Show of Shows* scripts. But like a certain shy schoolboy, Sid Caesar didn't exactly wear a *yarmulke* on air, right? In fact, *Your Show of Shows* writers Carl Reiner and Mel Brooks purposely kept their "most Jewish" bit to themselves. Their riotous "2000-Year-Old-Man" act remained an improvisational routine they performed only at private parties. In 1961, the pair recorded the hysterically funny bits for posterity only after encouragement from friends like showbiz big shot Steve Allen.[4] (While not Jewish himself, humor connoisseur Steve Allen famously declared that "all comics are Jewish!")

It wasn't until Lenny Bruce came along in the late 1950s that Jewish comics started wearing their religion on their tuxedo sleeves. Consider one of Bruce's routines about Jesus: "A lot of people say to me, 'Why did you kill Christ?' I dunno…It was one of those parties, got out of hand, you know…We killed him because he didn't want to become a doctor. That's why we killed him."[5]

But as that famous example suggests, the Lenny Bruce persona was still part-aggressive, part-apologetic, continuing the well-established traditions of the Catskills.

Then "ethnic pride" swept across America in the

1960s and 1970s, and Jewish Americans got caught up in the zeitgeist. Nose jobs became less popular during the 1970s, after Barbra Streisand became a superstar and role model, her big voice accompanied by a defiantly "unfixed" proboscis. The so-called Jewfro—the Jewish version of the then-popular African American afro hair-style, with its natural "halo" of curls—also made its de-but in the same decade.

Meanwhile, performers Jackie Mason and Woody Allen mined a rich vein of Jewish-but-embarrassed-about-it humor, with great success. Whereas Bruce's routines had been confined to audiences of hipsters in tiny night-clubs, Allen and other Jewish stand-ups in the 1960s and 1970s moved from clubs to TV and movies with rela tive ease, and were embraced by mainstream audiences. Their personas were less aggressive and confrontational than Bruce's, but they retained their Jewish "attitude" and cultural reference points. These comics adopted a psych-out survival strategy that involved hating your-self before the *goyim* got the chance—a kind of Jewish jujitsu—Jew-jitsu.

Woody Allen in particular became synonymous with Jewish comedy during the 1970s and 1980s. In hit films like *Play It Again, Sam* (1972)[6] he embodied the general public's indelible stereotype of the urban, secular Jewish *nebbish*. In his Oscar-winning classic *Annie Hall* (1977),[7] the title character's bigoted super-WASP grandmother imagines Allen sitting at their dinner table as a Hassid, complete with forelocks and black hat. Her hateful rev-erie is broken when Allen's character looks up from his plate and tries unsuccessfully to endear himself to the family by declaring, "This is dynamite ham."

At the same time, Mel Brooks came into his own with his considerably less sophisticated cinematic offerings. His Hollywood parodies, *Blazing Saddles*[8] and *Young Franken- stein*[9] both debuted in 1974, and starred two of Brooks' favorite collaborators, actors Madeline Kahn and Gene Wilder. Other than *Blazing*'s Yiddish-speaking Indian chief (played by Brooks himself) whose headdress reads "Kosher for Passover," Jewish content in these films was limited to sing-song verbal cadences and the occasional Yiddish slang words.

At one time, the number of comedy clubs in America could be counted on (maybe) two hands. All that changed during the "comedy boom" of the 1980s, as stand-up comedy and improv clubs started springing up all over the country (though some were nothing more than stupidly named, glorified strip mall restaurants hoping to discover the next big star). Gilbert Gottfried, Roseanne Barr, Carol Leifer and countless others got their start (and in the case of less talented or less ambitious stand-ups, their well-deserved finish) playing to hostile, boozy audiences.

By the time the 1990s came along, the "comedy boom" bubble had burst (although these clubs remain a staple of Los Angeles nightlife to this day). Many comedians, like Al Franken, had already moved on to "real" gigs on *Saturday Night Live* or the steady, well-paying college and corporate stand-up circuit. Meanwhile, Adam Sandler and Garry Shandling brought their distinctive—if not necessarily explicit—Jewish sensibility to sitcoms, sketch comedy and stand-up.

As time went on, TV characters like Kyle Broflovski (*South Park*), Fran Fine (*The Nanny*), Ross Geller (*Friends*), Dr. Joel Fleischman (*Northern Exposure*) and Grace Adler (*Will & Grace*) added more kosher flavor to the mix (as documented in Vincent Brook's book *Something Ain't Kosher Here: The Rise of the "Jewish" Sitcom*[10]). But when contemplating the quintessence of late twentieth-century Jewish comedy, one name wins by a (big) nose: Jerry Seinfeld.

During *Seinfeld*'s nine-season run (1989–1998), it became one of the most popular shows in television history. Its characters, situations and catchphrases (like "yadda yadda yadda") became cultural currency. Not surprisingly, the program also marked a turning point in the history of American Jewish humor. It was as if pioneers from Fanny Brice to Woody Allen had paved the way for these twenty-two-minutes-a-week with Jerry and friends.

The "show about nothing" followed the mundane lives of Jerry Seinfeld, a stand-up comic, and his underemployed, self-absorbed friends: George Costanza (Jason Alexander), Elaine Benes (Julia Louis-Dreyfus) and Cosmo Kramer (Michael Richards)—and his one nemesis, Newman (Wayne Knight). *Seinfeld* was set in an apartment block on Manhattan's Upper West Side, that neighborhood having replaced the legendary Lower East Side as New York City's (and the world's) unofficial Jewish capital.

The *Seinfeld* story lines were as shallow as the show's characters: a fruitless search for a car in a massive parking lot, the unwelcome gift of a "puffy" men's shirt or the horrors of dating a woman with "man hands." Naturally, these barely-there situations were just an excuse for the characters to *kvetch* to brilliant comedic effect.

After the first few successful seasons, *Seinfeld*'s sensibility became more explicitly Jewish, and the show just got more and more popular. In an episode that seemed like a knowing wink to all the non-Jewish viewers who loved the program, Jerry's Gentile dentist converts to Judaism— "for the jokes!"

> *Jerry*: Elaine, the guy's Jewish two days, he's already making Jewish jokes.
>
> *Elaine*: So what? When someone turns twenty-one, they usually get drunk the first night.
>
> *Jerry*: Booze is not a religion.
>
> *Elaine*: Tell that to my father.[11]

The nation had "converted" to Jewish humor.

Indeed, millions of Americans embraced these neurotic urban characters, making *Seinfeld* a huge hit. Jerry's character was obviously Jewish but not explicitly so, sort of "Israel-lite." After decades spent watching Jewish performers like the Marx Brothers and Lenny Bruce, viewers just "knew" that George Costanza, regardless of his Italian surname, was supposed to be a stereotypically neurotic, klutzy New York Jew. (Kramer's character originally had the more explicitly Semitic surname "Hoffman").

Ironically, George's character was based on the show's very Jewish cocreator, Larry David, the show's head writer and executive producer for the first seven seasons. (A special feature on the Season 5 DVD collection, "Jason + Larry = George," explains Costanza's back story: His father is Catholic but his mother is Jewish. Not surprisingly, Costanza's parents on the show were played by Jewish performers Jerry Stiller and Estelle Harris.)

The breathtaking success of the *Seinfeld* "experiment" gave Larry David the creative freedom he needed to follow up with one of the most openly Jewish comedy series ever, *Curb Your Enthusiasm*.

This show took the *Seinfeld* sensibility to a radical extreme, just in time for the new millennium. America had assimilated Jewishness, Jewishness had assimilated America, and *Curb Your Enthusiasm* would exploit both realities.

Asked to compare his new show to *Seinfeld*, "the show about nothing," Larry David responded, "I would describe it [*Curb Your Enthusiasm*] as a show about Larry David, which is pretty close to nothing, as it is."[12] Even so, that "nothing" possessed an explicitly Jewish flavor that *Seinfeld* never had. Specifically, *Curb* has explored American Jewry's love-hate relationship with the key struggles of contemporary Jewish life: assimilation, materialism and religion.

Curb Your Enthusiasm concerns the actual (more or less) off-screen life of Larry David. Post-*Seinfeld*, the wealthy, successful (and mostly miserable) David is now semiretired, having left the Upper West Side for glamorous Brentwood, Los Angeles. He hangs out with his manager Jeff Greene (Jeff Garlin) and Jeff's wife Susie (Susie Essman) and lives with his wife Cheryl (Cheryl Hines). (At least, he did, until an unfortunate incident with the TiVo repairman...)

Curb is truly the first twenty-first-century comedy. The absence of old-fashioned laugh tracks adds an uncomfortable silence to the painful spectacles unfolding before viewers' eyes. The show is shot with hand-held cameras, in the spirit of informal reality television or a homemade documentary. The resulting jerkiness furthers a sense of discomfort, making the viewers feel as awkward as the lead character. Most important, *Curb* dispenses with a traditional script. Each episode is expertly improvised around a loosely mapped-out story line. These elements, when combined, give *Curb* a "seat of our pants" energy that audiences either love or loathe.

Like those original *Seinfeld* cohorts, Larry David is a rude, self-centered *kvetcher*, obsessed with bizarre, pointless minutiae (really, who cares who invented the Cobb salad?). It's obvious from his character's persona that achieving the American dream hasn't made Larry David very happy. What Larry lacks in depth and sensitivity he makes up for with blunt, cringe-inducing candor: *Curb*'s original viewers either switched off in disgust or couldn't turn away from Larry's obnoxious antics.

More than a few of *Curb*'s plots and themes revolve around Jewish holidays, celebrations and locales, like kosher delis, Passover *seders*, bat mitzvahs and synagogues. Larry is proudly Jewish, albeit in his own distinctive way, telling his Gentile wife at Christmastime that "there's nothing worse than Jews with trees."

Curb openly celebrates, even exaggerates, something that is normally discussed in guilty whispers. Hollywood in general, and Larry's Brentwood in particular, is a bastion of Jewishness. *Curb*'s Jews are happy to be identified as members of the tribe. A stellar cast of Jewish celebrities make cameo appearances, including: Jason Alexander, David Schwimmer, Ben Stiller, Jerry Seinfeld, Joan Rivers, Bob Einstein, Gina Gershon, Susan Stroman, Rob Reiner, Shelly Berman, Mayim Bialik, Laraine Newman, Paul Mazursky, Mel Brooks, U.S. senator Barbara Boxer (D-Calif.) and Paul Reiser.[13]

Even heaven is apparently dominated by Jews—in Larry's world, Dustin Hoffman and Sasha Baron Cohen portray angels.

Of course, Hollywood is largely a Jewish creation, and Larry David plays up this fact to great comic effect. But for those original, foreign-born Hollywood pioneers— Carl Laemmle (Universal Pictures), Adolph Zukor (Paramount Pictures), William Fox (Fox Pictures, later named 20th Century Fox), Louis B. Mayer (Metro-Goldwyn-Mayer), Harry, Jack, Albert and Sam Warner (Warner Brothers)—who launched their studios in the 1910s and 1920s, their ethnic identity was an outright embarrassment. They took up the most WASPish of upper-class sports, polo. They made Danny Kaye dye his hair a non-Jewish shade of blond. And they bankrolled overtly Christian films like *The Sign of the Cross* (1932), *The Song of Bernadette* (1943) and *Easter Parade* (1948).

As Neal Gabler explained in *An Empire of Their Own: How the Jews Invented Hollywood*, the Jewish moguls built those studios without publicizing their religious background or communal affiliations. As Gabler writes, "They wanted to be regarded as Americans, not Jews." These innovators were united not by their shared faith and culture but by "an absolute rejection of their pasts and their equally absolute devotion to their new country."[14]

To generations of moviegoers, the studios' imaginary "white bread" vision of America became more "real" than reality. "By creating their idealized America on the screen," says Gabler, "the Jews reinvented the country in the image of their fiction."[15] From the wholesome Andy Hardy series and glittering Busby Berkeley musicals to unforgettable classics like *Gone With the Wind* and *The Wizard of Oz*, identifiably Jewish characters were absent in this celluloid America.

Such self-censorship reflected painful memories of deadly European pogroms and experiences with American anti-Semitism, which arose during the wave of mass immigration in the late nineteenth and early twentieth centuries, peaking in the Great Depression. Interestingly, growing awareness of what happened in Europe during the Holocaust helped reduce overt anti-Semitism in America. The first two Hollywood films to tackle American anti-Semitism, *Crossfire*[16] and *Gentleman's Agreement*[17] (both 1947, and both produced and directed by non-Jews), were made after knowledge of the Holocaust had become widespread.

The persistent absence of Jewish characters spread beyond the movie theater. In *The Jews of Prime Time*, David Zurawik writes: "Just as the tension between Jewish identity and assimilation on the part of studio bosses and producers manifested itself when it came to Jewish images on the big screen—especially in the matter of suppressing such images—so it did on the smaller screen of television."[18]

In just one of many examples, Zurawik recounts the famous memo sent out by CBS executives, confidently informing producers back in the 1950s that American viewers did not want to see "divorced people[...]people from New York, men with mustaches, and Jews."[19] Fortunately, Jerry Seinfeld wasn't around to pitch his sitcom in those days!

What led to the increase in acceptance we take for granted today? Zurawik notes that in the mid-1980s, the old-time TV moguls (with their built-in prejudices) sold their empires to corporate conglomerates, who may not have been any more enlightened, but who knew what audiences wanted and what generated profits. Granted, other social phenomena were at work, too. The dramatic events of the second half of the twentieth century paved the way for an all-around openness to cultural and religious differences, on- and off-screen. The impact of the civil rights movements of the 1960s, the ethnic pride phenomenon of the 1970s, the political correctness of the 1980s, and the de rigueur multiculturalism of the 1990s cannot be ignored.

However, "all around" doesn't necessarily mean "universal." In the film *For Your Consideration* (2006), an indie film-within-a-film is retitled to satisfy non-Jewish viewers. *Home for Purim* becomes *Home for Thanksgiving*. As the studio exec played by Ricky Gervais suggests, "Tone down the Jewishness so everybody can enjoy it. Have it there but don't shove it down everybody's throat. I don't go around saying 'I'm a Gentile.'"[20] Lines like that show how far we've come from the days of TV execs banning "men with mustaches" to safeguard the real or imaginary sensibilities of American audiences. Gervais is not a real studio executive and *Home for Purim* isn't an actual movie, so the film's "Jewishness" isn't really being "toned down" at all. By raising the issue for the sake of a punch line, the creators of *For Your Consideration* (i.e., Jewish director and co-writer Christopher Guest) are in fact "toning it up."

The status that was so long-desired has been achieved, and the disguising of Jewishness that took place in Hollywood's early days is now part of the joke. *Curb* suggests that Hollywood's carefully constructed, dreamy WASP fantasies are actually manufactured by status-obsessed Jewish therapy junkies, caught up in foolish petty squabbles, always jockeying for some dubious position or award. It's become the stuff of a new wave of Jewish comedy.

Due to the years of self-censorship, this "outing" of Jews in showbiz has become a parlor game popularized most famously by Adam Sandler's 1994 "Chanukah Song," which revealed, to the astonishment of goyim everywhere (and most Jews), that among others, Harrison Ford and David Lee Roth were members of the tribe. The song was such a hit that Sandler produced multiple sequels; the version Sandler performs in the animated movie *Eight Crazy Nights* (2002) includes a lyric about Osama bin Laden, who's "Not a big fan of the Jews / Because he lost the figure skating match to Jewish gold medalist Sarah Hughes!"[21]

Demonstrating the contemporary openness about Jewish identity, the 2006 book *Stars of David* by Abigail Pogrebin also intellectualized the concept. The book features interviews with more than sixty celebrities discussing their Jewish identities. Of course, not everybody in Hollywood is Jewish, yet even non-Jewish celebrities seem eager to embrace the faith, or at least, its trendy

Kabbalah incarnation. In fact, lots of people assume that non-Jewish celebrities, particularly comedians, must be Jews. Catholic-raised Dennis Miller laughs about getting Chanukah cards from the White House every year.

Today's Jewish comics aren't afraid of proclaiming their ethnicity. Nor are they desperate to apologize for who they are. They are being themselves for better or worse, and have the confidence to laugh about their frailties. The understated "Jew-*ish*" flavor of *Seinfeld* and its predecessors has been replaced by a brutal matter-of-factness that would make earlier generations of Jewish comics cringe.

I call this new comic sensibility *the shtick shift*.

Part of what makes these new comedians such skilled commentators are the ways they shine a spotlight on their Jewish identities instead of disguising them.

Take Jon Stewart's wildly popular *The Daily Show*—he sometimes complains when guests "go all Jewy." *Borat* creator Sacha Baron Cohen calls upon others to "shoot the Jew" or "throw the Jew down the well." Both performers are firmly rooted in reality—or at least a twisted sense of reality that includes themselves in their parody of anti-Semitism. All very post-postmodern.

Unlike their comedic ancestors, Jewish comedians of the twenty-first century don't play down or apologize for their heritage. They offer fresh perspectives on familiar themes in Jewish humor: money, family, faith, politics and bigotry. Their humor may not be subtle, and it often exhibits a bitter, twisted edge. But at least it is honest, sometimes brutally. *Shtick Shift* aims for the same level of honesty. We'll look frankly at what the new generation of Jewish comics have to say about contemporary Jewish life, and vice-versa.

Living in a time of unprecedented assimilation, in which ethnic groups in America are protected by law from discrimination and civil rights are a given, a new question arises. If Jewish humor was originally a response to oppression, what happens when the oppression largely disappears? What are the consequences when the only suffering that remains is neurosis, self-hatred or the "responsibilities" of being rich and famous? If Larry David is any indication, Jews still feel rotten.

It's a situation that reflects Americans on the whole. The wealthiest and most powerful nation in history is sorely hurting for a laugh about its own (mis)fortunes. Their grandparents may have survived the Holocaust, but will post–9/11 Jewish comics, who've never experienced violent persecution firsthand, be able to rise to serious challenges?

Shtick Shift explores these themes, with plenty of humor and a sprinkling of spirituality (what else did you expect from a rabbi?). Think of *Shtick Shift* as your primer to the ever-changing face of Jewish comedy at the dawn of the twenty-first century: The new faces, their outrageous routines and their sometimes surprising seriousness about the most (de)pressing issues of our time.

And now: On with the show...

"1"

JEW GOLD: SELF-FULFILLING STEREOTYPES AND UNFULFILLING WEALTH

Cartman: Hand over the gold!
Kyle: What gold??
Cartman: You know what I'm talking about!
Kyle: No, Cartman, I have no idea what you're talking about!
Cartman: All Jews carry gold in a little bag around their necks![1]

Like the best *South Park* bits, the one above is so twisted it doubles back on itself. In this episode of Comedy Central's subversive adult cartoon, Kyle's boorish pal Cartman is demanding that Kyle hand over his "Jew gold"—a bag of treasure that Cartman is convinced all Jewish brethren secretly keep around their necks.

In this scene's "shtick shift," the idiotic Cartman turns out to be right for once: Kyle really has such a bag!

Cartman isn't satisfied, though.

"Do you think I'm stupid?!" he whines. "I know that all Jews carry fake bags of gold around their necks to keep the real bags of gold around their necks safe! Hand over the real Jew gold, Kyle!"

And sure enough, not only does Kyle have a bag of gold, he's got a decoy, too.

Stereotypes and urban legends about money and Jews die hard, perhaps because they got their start centuries ago. Since biblical times, Jews have been publicly engaged in financial transactions—and the complex and paradoxical relationship Jews have with money goes back almost that far. Stereotypes of Jews as dirty money-grubbers were commonplace in medieval and Renaissance Europe, when Jewish people weren't permitted to own property or enter "respectable" professions. They were, however, allowed to lend money at interest, which was then considered a mortal sin by their Christian and Muslim neighbors. Non-Jewish rulers enjoyed all the benefits of usury while hypocritically damning the very same Jews who financed their endeavors. How convenient.

In the phrase coined by sociologist Edna Bonocich, Jews around the world became a middleman minority "standing between the peasant and the king, playing the role of middleman between producer and consumer, employer and employee, owner and renter, elite and masses."[2] Literary giants Shakespeare and Dickens immortalized Jews as societal enemies with their controversial outsider characters Shylock and Fagin.

Across the pond, American Jewish prosperity emerged from grinding poverty. According to economist Thomas Sowell, "A 1908 study found that about half the families on the Lower East Side slept three or four people to a room, nearly one-fourth slept five or more to a room, and fewer than one-fourth slept two to a room."[3]

In those days, the Lower East Side teemed with pushcarts overflowing with cheap clothing, kitchen utensils and sundries, and food of every kind. Some merchants saved enough to open their own little shops, offering every type of merchandise imaginable to their bargain-hunting neighbors. Incredibly, all these experiences—

of extreme victimization, tyranny and appalling poverty—led to raucous comedy.

As we noted in the Introduction, Jewish vaudeville stars of the early twentieth century were among the impoverished children of an estimated two million desperate Jewish immigrants. The Marx Brothers' misbegotten upbringing became part of their legend, and in his memoir, Harpo recalled the adventures of "Minnie's boys" in their crowded apartment: "But thanks to the amazing spirit of my mother and father, poverty never made any of us depressed or angry. My memory of my earliest years is vague but pleasant, full of the sound of singing and laughter, and full of people I loved."[4]

In time, complicated feelings about money, success and security inevitably burrowed into the comedy routines of these early American performers. Jack Benny, for instance, made a hugely successful career out of the "Jewish cheapskate" persona, although the "Jewish" element was implied rather than explicit. Invited to throw out the first ball at the World Series, Benny played to the stereotype by pocketing the ball and sitting down. In one of his most famous radio routines, a thief holds up Benny at gunpoint and growls, "Your money or your life!" After repeated threats and a painfully long pause, Benny finally replies, "I'm thinking, I'm thinking…" By that point his audiences, who were all too familiar with the comic's penny-pinching persona, had already collapsed in laughter anticipating the punch line.

Benny's contemporary counterpart is Jeremy Piven's aptly named Ari Gold, the Hollywood agent from HBO's *Entourage* (said to be based on real-life Endeavor agent

Ari Emanuel, who represents actor and series producer Mark Wahlberg). Ari is that abrasively rude guy we've all put up with, yacking on his cell phone in the restaurant about his "very important dealings," while pretending he's oblivious to the negative attention he attracts.

He's not evil so much as annoying. Ari can be petty, ruthless, insensitive, and materialistic, yet he cares deeply for his family, and at times his insecurity betrays his bulletproof shell.

In a recent episode of *Entourage*, Ari is trying to broker a film deal—but the sunset deadline coincides with Yom Kippur. Later, when Ari attempts to negotiate with an Orthodox studio head in the middle of services, he comments: "This is time-sensitive. God will understand."[5] If Ari doesn't succeed, he'll soon be on the receiving end of such scorn by another such "Ari" and he knows it. His success represents the mirror opposite of that earlier generation of assimilated Jews who turned poverty into comedy. And yet the portrayal is as unflattering as the old stereotype.

Raised in an atmosphere of relative security, confidence and success, only "shock" comedy seems to touch the jaded funny bones of today's Jewish youth. Could, or would, Fanny Brice ever sing, as Sarah Silverman does, "I love you more than Jews love money"? Silverman and her contemporaries appear determined to beat anti-Semites to the punch (line). When once they laughed about poverty, now they laugh about money. In both cases, the key issue is security—something that has always concerned Jews.[6]

Sacha Baron Cohen became a multi-millionaire, in part, by making jokes about the fabled Jewish obsession

with money. He also became a lightning rod for controversy and lawsuits in his portrayal of a fictional Kazakh
reporter who believes Jews are money-grubbing, shape-
shifting demons. In his blockbuster comedy *Borat: Cultural Learnings of America for Make Benefit Glorious Nation
of Kazakhstan* (2006), Cohen and his on-screen producer
take a room in a bed & breakfast run by a harmless old
Jewish couple. Cowering in their room at night, the guests
throw dollar bills at cockroaches slipping under the door,
believing the pests are their hosts in disguise. Within seconds, they bolt out the door declaring that they should
have stayed in New York, "where there are no Jews."

Just a few years ago, the mere concept of a publi-
cation called *Heeb* was unimaginable. But in the same
myth-busting irreverent spirit of Sacha Baron Cohen
and Sarah Silverman, the hip and often controversial
youth magazine of that name has found a readership. In
the spring of 2006, *Heeb* unveiled its Money issue. The
magazine's editor explained the rationale behind the issue was "not simply to revel in the fact that Jews are the
wealthiest ethnic group in America today, nor to roman-
ticize a past when Jews were still outsiders, but to create
a conversation about what money means to Jews and
Jews to money today."[7] Along with some think pieces,
the issue featured a "Jewish Media Monopoly" board,
with Park Place and Boardwalk replaced by Dream-
Works and Marvel Comics. It's almost as if the subject
of Jews and money can't be broached (at least by Jews)
without some levity to offset it.

No one embodies the theme of Jews and money in
the twenty-first century better than *Curb Your Enthusiasm*'s
Larry David.

In an essay called "Can Jewish-American Humor Survive the Assimilationist 21st Century?," Professor Sanford Pinsker wonders if Jewish humor can flourish much longer in an atmosphere of material success and security, absent the motivation of oppression and poverty. Fear not, Pinsker answers. "*Curb Your Enthusiasm* makes it clear, week after week, that an annoyingly funny millionaire curmudgeon can also be a *schlemiel*."[8]

Much like Ari Gold's character on *Entourage*, Larry David is often caught up in the complications of security and money. But whereas Ari Gold needs money to displace his anxiety, Larry neurotically frets over success. Larry's dilemmas are a long way from *Fiddler on the Roof*, where the hero, Tevye, plaintively sang "If I Were a Rich Man," and the ins and outs of wealth management weren't exactly a pressing issue. The mordant humor in *Fiddler* and other *shtetl* stories reflects a fatalism brought on by grinding, inescapable poverty and persecution. And the way contemporary Jewish humor engages Jewish stereotypes head-on by embodying them shares this older fatalism. If contemporary Jews seem fated to be stereotyped as wealthy, Jewish comedy makes that wealth awkward and problematic. Larry *is* a rich man, but he's still miserable.

Saul Bellow once observed, "Oppressed people tend to be witty."[9] As we've noted, Jewish humor is rooted in the hardscrabble experiences of immigrant Jews from Eastern Europe who settled in New York City a century ago. But for twenty-first-century American Jews like Larry David, the oppression is where, exactly?

After all, Larry's Brentwood is a fairyland-*shtetl* of chic clothing boutiques, exclusive restaurants and coffee shops, therapists and acupuncturists. Extravagant—but not terribly welcoming—country clubs are a particularly popular setting on the show, as befits their ambiguous place in American Jewish culture. In one episode, Larry is suspended from his private golf club for a multitude of sins, including having a dirty locker, mistaking a Norwegian club employee for a Swede and acting disrespectfully at a funeral. Desperate to regain their prestige in the community, Larry and his wife pretend to be right-wing Republican WASPs in order to join another country club.[10] The scene is reminiscent of Groucho Marx's famous line (which has, tellingly, become one of the most quoted Jewish jokes of all time), reiterated by Woody Allen in *Annie Hall*: "I would never belong to any club that would have someone like me as a member."

Brentwood turns out to be nothing more than an upscale version of Chelm, the fabled village of fools from Jewish folklore, but in this town, the *schlemiels* and *schnorrers* wear Versace. Like the popular old television series *The Beverly Hillbillies, Curb Your Enthusiasm* reinforces the importance of one's origins and the impossibility of ever really getting away from your roots. You can take the Jews out of the *shtetl,* but you can't take the *shtetl* out of the Jews. Left with nothing real to be angry or passionate about, Larry picks fights with friends like actors David Schwimmer and Ben Stiller (more or less playing themselves) about the most trivial things, from the "cashew-raisin balance" in a line of snacks to the subtle difference between "dry" and "wet" sneezes and the etiquette they demand.

Larry's misery is shared by his on-and-off "best friend," comedian Richard Lewis, who plays his deeply neurotic self. The pair are two stock characters from *shetl* stories. When Larry, the *schlemiel,* spills the soup, it always lands on Richard, the *schlemazel.*

Naturally, Larry and Richard also share an obsession with psychotherapy—but again: What do these two rich and famous men have to be so depressed about? Clearly Jewish comics need no excuse to hire a shrink; the psychotherapist is a modern-day stock character in Jewish comedy, hovering in the background as both straight man and status symbol. The obsession was mutual: Sigmund Freud famously wrote a deeply unfunny book exploring comedy and the unconscious mind, and observed about Jews: "I do not know whether there are many other instances of a people making fun to such a degree of its own character."[11]

Larry's frantic obsession with insignificant trivia distracts him from dwelling too much on his deep insecurities, whether he's on the shrink's couch or not. He seems guilty about having made his fortune in the glamorous, superficial world of showbiz. Thanks to his patronizing attempts at solidarity with "ordinary people," millionaire Larry offends waiters, secretaries and retail clerks wherever he goes. At one point Larry asks a Starbucks employee, "What's in a latte?" When the employee replies, "Milk and coffee," Larry condescendingly feigns surprise, "I would never, *would never* have thought of that! That's so brilliant."[12]

Larry's real problem is a terminal case of "affluenza," brought on by the contrast between his relatively modest upbringing and his current good fortune. Those guilty feelings manifest themselves in his twitchy, touchy, self-centered persona. Larry is incapable of simply relaxing and enjoying his success.

It's a lesson well illustrated by a famous Hassidic story concerning the eighteenth-century Polish Hassidic leader, Rabbi Levi Yitzhak of Berditchev. Looking out over the town square, he sees people rushing everywhere. He calls out to one man, "What are you rushing for?" The man replied, "I'm running to make a living." The rabbi asks, "What makes you so sure that your livelihood is in front of you so that you have to rush to catch it up? What if it's behind you? Maybe you should stop and let it catch up with you."[13]

The real irony is that unlike most other religions, Judaism doesn't look askance at material success or ambition *prima facie*. Eskimos are said to have a hundred words for snow. Likewise, the Jewish obsession with failure is also reflected in the large number of Yiddish words—many of which have been absorbed into the English language—denoting losers and idiots: *shlemiel, shlemazel, shmendrik, shmo* and *nebbish*.[14]

Not surprisingly, the Torah contains many teachings on the purpose of wealth. Great riches, the sages taught, can trap the wealthy when they lead them away from loftier goals. In the biblical story of the Exodus, the Jewish people escape from slavery in Egypt bearing tremendous wealth and fulfilling a promise made many years before to Avraham: "And also that nation, whom they shall serve, will I judge; and afterward shall they come out with great wealth" (Genesis 15:14).

These riches are earmarked to build the Tabernacle—the portable, temporary focal point of the refugees' spirituality while they wander the desert. But the people get restless. Unmoored by their newfound freedom, overwhelmed by the desert's emptiness and believing Moses has abandoned them, the Jews long for something they can see and touch. Eventually, they waste their treasure by creating an idol in the form of a golden calf, fashioning a cursed abomination with riches intended as a blessing.

South Park's jabs at "Jew gold" remind us of a greater, more serious truth: our obligation to use our "gold" for its intended holy purpose. When we give to charity, for example, we elevate our riches to their rightful place. Getting and spending merely to keep up appearances is no better than building a cold, useless idol in the middle of an empty wasteland. Hoarding our gold "around our necks" (as it were) creates a burden on us, and keeps it from being a blessing to others.

Despite the old stereotype of the "cheap" Jew, Judaism places great emphasis on charitable giving. The Talmud notes that charity is actually equal to all the other commandments combined (Talmud, Bava Basra 9a). While the word *tzedakah* is most commonly translated into English as "charity," it actually comes from the Hebrew word meaning "justice" or "righteousness." In other words, philanthropy is more than just an optional "good deed"—it's the absolute duty of every righteous man and woman.

For some Jews, charitable giving is indeed a difficult goal. Despite the persistent perceptions that all Jewish people are rich, the 2004 *Report on Jewish Poverty,* commissioned by the Metropolitan Council on Jewish Poverty and the UJA-Federation of New York, discovered that almost 20 percent of New York Jews were living in poverty.[15] In Brooklyn alone, nearly one-third of its 516,000 Jewish inhabitants had household incomes under 150 percent of the Federal Poverty Guideline—a 54 percent increase in Brooklyn's poor Jewish population over the previous decade. For a family of four, we're talking an annual income of $27,000—in New York City. One would be hard-pressed to get by on that in Sioux City, let alone New York City. For every Larry David and Ari Gold living in relative luxury, there's a young Marx brother trying to scrape by.

On the other side of the coin, so to speak, *Business Week's* 2006 list of "The 50 Most Generous Philanthropists" includes at least fifteen Jews.[16] That's pretty impressive in light of the fact that Jews make up only about 2 percent of the American population. And this generosity extends beyond Jewish charities: Most philanthropists in that "Top 50" list give to Jewish and non-Jewish charities alike. Obviously, all those stereotypes about rich but stingy Jews don't reflect the whole truth.

Leave it to Larry David to make even something positive like giving to charity something to *kvetch* at. In the episode tellingly titled "The Anonymous Donor," Larry gives money to a real-life environmental group called the Natural Resources Defense Council. At a party celebrating the donors' generosity, Larry is *kvelling* at seeing his name in the place of honor on a wall plaque at NRDC headquarters. The crowd, however, is more impressed with the plaque on the opposite wall, which simply states "Anonymous." If the frequent whispers of the crowd are believed, that donor is actually actor Ted Danson, leading Larry to condemn Danson's "faux anonymity" as "fake philanthropy."[17] When it comes to money, it seems Larry just can't win.

Larry is a lot of things, but a *mensch* isn't one of them.

Being called a *mensch*—a decent, generous, charitable fellow—is one of the highest compliments any Jew can receive. So it's ironic that a particularly lovable example of *mensch*-iness almost wasn't allowed to show his face on TV. Just as a ventriloquist's cartoonish dummy can vocalize insults that would earn the ventriloquist himself a punch in the nose, all of the "harmless-looking" adult animated comedies so popular today can get away with things a live-action program never could. Usually. But one notorious episode of the unfailingly offensive show *Family Guy* (another tasteless adult cartoon in the spirit of *South Park*) wasn't aired until three years after it was produced, precisely because it skewered a host of clichés with even more blatant disregard for propriety than usual. Not surprisingly, the episode's writer, Ricky Blitt, is Jewish.

In "When You Wish Upon a Weinstein," hero Peter Griffin squanders the *family's* rainy day fund on "volcano insurance" (don't ask) and his wife contemplates divorcing him for a monkey who makes more money (ditto). Influenced by friends who've been discussing the supposed financial acumen peculiar to "members of the tribe," Peter figures he needs a Jew to fix his money woes.[18]

He latches onto the first one he sees—Max Weinstein, a total stranger whose car breaks down outside Peter's house.

> *Max:* Hi. My name's Max Weinstein. My car just broke down. May I use your phone?
>
> *Peter:* Now my troubles are all through—I have a Jew.
>
> *Max:* Hey!

Peter: I prayed for you, Max Weinstein, and here you are.

Max: Okay. Listen, uh, thanks for letting me use the phone.

Peter: Thanks for *Spaceballs.*

Max: If there's anything I can do for you…

Peter: You can't leave!

Max: What do you want?

Peter: Financial advice.

Max: Financial advice? How the hell did you know I'm an accountant?

Peter: Hello! 'Max Weinstein?'

Max: Look, I'll do what I can, but I don't know why you think I can get your money back.

Peter: Max, Max, Max! Let's not deny our heritages. You're Jewish, you're good with money.[19]

Peter's family accompanies Max the *mensch* to his Reform synagogue ("Temple Beth Supporting Actor"). For Peter, it's an eye-opening experience: "Hey, look! I didn't know the principal of Meg's school was Jewish. Hey, there's Bill Nye, the Science Guy, and half of Lenny Kravitz. Optimus Prime? He's Jewish?"[20]

Peter is so impressed he tries to make his son convert thinking it will improve the boy's grades. Luckily, Peter comes to his senses by the end of the show.

Peter: I'm sorry, Lois. I just wanted our son to be Jewish so he'd be smarter. Then maybe his wife wouldn't be sorry she didn't marry the chimp next door.

Lois: Oh, Peter, just because Steven makes more money than you doesn't mean he's any smarter. And I think Chris will do just fine.

Peter: How do you know that?

Lois: Because I have faith in him, the way I have faith in you. Besides, a person's religion is no guarantee of success.

Peter: I see what you're saying. The Jews are just like us. No better, no worse.

Chris: Yeah, and as they say, *'Zahl zine mit glick.'*

Lois: What?

Peter: I think what he's trying to say is everything's gonna be okay.

Cutting-edge, contemporary comedies can convey classic teachings: There is no real connection between wealth and happiness (nor between an ethnicity and its material wealth). Sure, we'd all love to have a little more money, maybe even a lot more. But wealth comes at a price. In fact, *Ethics of the Fathers* famously states, "Who is the rich person? One who takes joy in his lot." (4:1) Whether Jewish comedians are making fun of poverty or wealth, the one thing the comedy imparts is the necessity to laugh with awareness. Poverty and wealth are really just symptoms of security; if you can turn your symptoms into comedy, then you're not controlled by the symptoms—you control *them.*

Unfortunately, not everyone has gotten the message that money can't buy you happiness. And when extravagant spending and conspicuous consumption collides with spirituality, the results are hilarious, but troubling.

" 🗣 2 "

RAISING THE BAR: BLING MITZVAH

"It doesn't matter what happens in the Temple,
it's the party that counts."
—Keeping Up with the Steins *(2006)*[1]

A majestic *Queen Mary*–style ocean liner in all its glory proudly displays a massive banner that reads, "*Mazel Tov*, Zachary!"

Inside, the crowd quiets down as canned music revs up on cue. Then a dramatic voice intones: "In 1912, the *Titanic* set sail. In 1997, the movie *Titanic* came out. And in 2006, Zachary has a *Titanic*-themed bar mitzvah!"

The morbid irony of linking a Jewish boy's rite of passage to a doomed ship that sank on its maiden voyage is clearly lost on thirteen-year-old Zachary. The (newly minted) man of the moment beams as he makes his big entrance to the party, *his* party, on a massive mock-up of the *Titanic*. Of course, Zachary is draped over the mast, just like Leonardo DiCaprio in the blockbuster movie. For purposes of authenticity, a hired model plays the part of Kate Winslet. But she's just another prop. Zachary, the bar mitzvah boy, is the day's one and only star.

The accompanying show rivals a glitzy Las Vegas production, complete with scantily clad "mermaids." Then, during the big finish, a massive polystyrene iceberg crashes into the fake *Titanic*. Zachary quickly steadies himself, and then delivers his big, well-rehearsed line in a less than impressive, high-pitched squeak: "Today, I'm the king of the Torah!" As the crowd of well wishers roars its approval, Zachary sees his chance and plants a big kiss on the model's lips.

A *Titanic*-themed bar mitzvah—have we Jews really sunk so low? What happened to our zaydes' tales of wine, sponge cake and that fabled fountain pen?

Don't worry, it's only a movie. Sort of. That tacky *Titanic* bar mitzvah provides the opening scene of the 2006 movie *Keeping Up with the Steins*. This family-friendly comedy is also a cautionary tale. In the movie, and increasingly in real life, parents hijack their sons' and daughters' bar and bat mitzvahs, trying to outdo each other in displays of garish opulence in which spirituality is drowned out by materialism and competitiveness.

(It isn't such a shtick shift: back in 1969, the film *Goodbye Columbus*—based on the 1959 novel by Philip Roth—featured a controversial wedding banquet scene that mocked nouveau riche excess.)

In the film, Zachary's father Arnie (Larry Miller) is *kvelling* in the *nachas* that "his" *Titanic* bar mitzvah is sure to dominate the season. (He has to explain to his *shiksa* trophy wife that the Yiddish word for joy—*nachas*—aren't those chips you serve with salsa.)

Arnie's former business partner, Adam (Jeremy Piven, in a less nasty version of the character he plays in *Entourage*[2]), whose own son's bar mitzvah is a few months away, feels pressure to outdo his old rival. As a big *macher* entertainment agent, Adam's in a position to stage the celebration of the new century. Adam's *nebbish* son Benjamin (Daryl Sabara) is needled into picking a baseball theme for his own party—so what else is there to do but rent out Dodgers Stadium? It's a full-frontal attack on the Steins, and the battle of the bar mitzvahs is on.

No doubt many real-life Jewish viewers will be cringing as they see themselves reflected in this too-close-for-comfort satire. These days, "many bar mitzvahs are grander than weddings—weddings often end in divorce, but bar mitzvahs last forever," explained one real-life veteran party planner, in a *New York* magazine cover story.[3]

An aquatic bar mitzvah like the one in *Keeping Up with the Steins* isn't just the far-out invention of a Hollywood screenwriter. For one real-life 1990s bat mitzvah, writer Ari L. Goldman highlights that "a hotel ballroom was transformed into a scene from the movie *Titanic*. There were twelve-foot steaming smoke stacks at the buffet tables, phosphorescent artificial icebergs, and a "steerage" section for the children. A gigantic photo, rising ten feet above the floor, featured Lisa's face superimposed over the actress Kate Winslet's body on the prow of the luxury liner, with Leonardo's DiCaprio smiling over her shoulder."[4] Sound familiar?

In the past few years, major news sources have covered lavish bar mitzvahs (and even more lavish bat mitzvahs) with a cynical wink. America's seemingly insatiable appetite for nostalgic kitsch means that the rich, famous and beautiful—who'd probably hidden away their cheesy bat and bar mitzvah photos for fear of being seen as they once were—are now comically "coming clean" about their own pasts. In *Mazel Tov: Celebrities' Bar and Bat Mitzvah Memories,* Hollywood's finest reveal the details of their own rites of passage with embarrassing candor.[5] It's a perfect example of postmodern Jews being forthright about their faith in a funny way.

In *Keeping Up with the Steins,* Adam's obsessive jealousy boils over while practicing tennis at his plush country club.[6] With his racket in one hand and cell phone in the other, he tries desperately to book notorious rap star 50 Cent for the event. Upon hearing the price tag, he responds, "Well, what about 25 cents?"

The joke is not as ludicrous as you may imagine. For the 2005 lavish bat mitzvah dubbed the "Mitzvahpalooza" by the New York *Daily News*—put on by Long Island defense contractor David H. Brooks in the glitzy Manhattan Rainbow Room—the rapper famous for declaring he'd "get rich or die trying" joined a well-paid line-up that would put the Grammys to shame: Aerosmith's Steven Tyler and Joe Perry; The Eagles' Don Henley and Joe Walsh; Fleetwood Mac's Stevie Nicks; rap diva Ciara; and even Kenny G. Maybe the singers were a little too old for the kids, who reportedly "seemed more impressed by their $1,000 gift bags, complete with digital cameras and the latest video iPod." Total cost: an estimated $10 million.[7]

In the 1970s and 1980s, the average guy's bar mitzvah was less glamorous, but still tacky in its own low-rent way. The 1970s bat mitzvah for the villain's daughter in *Starsky & Hutch* (2004) must have brought back unpleasant memories for more than a few viewers, with its hired mimes, Jewfro'd guests and a revolting singer who serenades the birthday girl with a sexually explicit pop song.[8]

The 2005 book *Bar Mitzvah Disco* by Roger Bennett, Nick Kroll, and Jules Shell, takes a nostalgic look at the real-life bar and bat mitzvahs from that misbegotten era, complete with embarrassing photos of boys in ugly polyester suits and thousands of dollars of orthodontics posing in the synagogue. (Maybe their parties would have been more lavish if the kids had been blessed with naturally straight teeth.) Among many other things, the book reveals that food, not religion, is the major issue on the big day:

"The buffet was a feeding frenzy in which a medium-sized smoked fish (with the bar mitzvah boy's name spelled on it in olives and pimentos) would be stripped to the bone in a time span that would make the most vicious shoal of piranha reach for the Pepto-Bismol."[9]

In the intervening years, at least the food seems to have improved. As Ralph Gardner Jr. observed in that *New York* magazine story, "Sushi is to baby-boomer-sponsored bar mitzvahs what chopped-liver molds were to their parents' generation."[10]

Scott Marshall, the director of *Keeping Up with the Steins*, has his own personal bar mitzvah angst—and he's not even Jewish.

"I did go to a school with a lot of Jewish children," he recalled. "I was always jealous of the big parties."[11] And he's not alone. In a 2004 *Wall Street Journal* article entitled, "You Don't Have to Be Jewish to Have a Bar Mitzvah," Elizabeth Bernstein revealed the latest iterations of bar and bat mitzvah envy when she spoke to a girl from a Methodist family who wanted to be Jewish so she could have a bat mitzvah. "A number of kids about to turn thirteen who aren't Jewish are bugging their parents for parties that resemble those held following bar mitzvah ceremonies," Bernstein claimed.[12] (It's an interesting reversal of the proverbial envy Jewish kids sometimes experience when their Christian friends celebrate Christmas.)

The following year a *Miami Herald* article took it even further: Not only do you not have to be Jewish to have a bar mitzvah, you apparently don't even have to be human. Welcome to the world of the Bark Mitzvah, the trendy K9 rite of passage. [13]

"Donning a gold yarmulke and a prayer shawl, thirteen-year-old Columbo, a toy poodle, marked his entry into the world as an adult." Surrounded by his best doggy friends, Columbo received a certificate—but not the traditional fountain pen. Columbo's owner noted, "This is a very important event in his life." Maybe he's inspired by the findings of a 2007 book, *How to Raise a Jewish Dog.*[14] Who knows? Maybe Columbo read it himself.

A more serious development is the celebration of a bar mitzvah later in life, for those who missed the opportunity at thirteen (e.g., those who came of age in the old Soviet Union, where religious practices were forbidden). Jews who survived such experiences are often able to appreciate this poignant occasion with greater maturity than their teenage counterparts.

Henny Youngman—the King of the One Liners—was a British-born Jewish American comedian and violinist, a beloved Borscht Belt star who kept them laughing right up to his death at age ninety-one. Youngman missed his own bar mitzvah as a boy when the death of his cousin canceled his big day. He ended up celebrating his bar mitzvah in his seventies, in a fitting venue for the quintessential Jewish stand-up and Carnegie Deli-habitué: Atlantic City. In his autobiography, *Take My Life, Please*, Youngman poignantly recalled, "I announced to the world at seventy-three, 'I am a man.'"[15]

Henny Youngman was not the only aging Jewish comic to become a man later in life. *The Simpsons'* very own Jewish comic, Krusty the Clown (aka Herschel Pinkus Yerucham Krustofski), got a bar mitzvah in the memorable 2003 episode, "Today I Am a Clown" (written by Joel H. Cohen).[16] It all starts when Krusty discovers he doesn't have a star on the Jewish Walk of Fame. He files a complaint at their head office ("Where the chosen get chosen" as the sign on the wall declares), and finds out that because he never had a bar mitzvah, he's not eligible for a star of his own.

Krusty is devastated. "I thought I was a self-hating Jew, but it turns out I'm just a plain old anti-Semite." Krusty visits his estranged Orthodox father, Rabbi Hyman Krustofski (memorably voiced by Jackie Mason), who is forever saddened that Krusty did not enter the family business of the rabbinate ("A jazz singer, this I could forgive. But a clown?").[17] Hyman tells Krusty that he decided to forgo the boy's bar mitzvah out of fear that his jokester son would "make a mockery out of the whole ceremony."

Determined to set things right, Krusty makes sacrifices in preparation for his long-delayed entrance into manhood. He cancels his Saturday show due to Sabbath observance and refuses to eat a (very *treif*) submarine sandwich that contains an entire pig's head. But it isn't easy for Krusty to change his ways.

Like the Steins, Krusty's bar mitzvah quickly becomes just a superficial circus, pitched to the Fox television network as "Krusty the Clown's Wet 'n' Wild Bar Mitzvah!" Mr. T joins in the *simcha* and gets to utter some of the funniest lines in bar mitzvah history: "I pity the *shul* that won't let Krusty in now!" "I pity the fool who didn't bring an envelope to this bar mitzvah!"

After the over-the-top TV special, Krusty celebrates a simpler, low-key bar mitzvah in his family's old synagogue, finally allowing his proud father to *schep* some *nachas.*

The words "bar mitzvah" literally mean "son of the commandments." The bar mitzvah boy has reached the age of maturity, and is no longer considered a child (but don't mention that to his *Bubbe*). He's now obligated to fulfill Jewish laws, take responsibility for his actions, and become more proactive in Jewish life. He can now don *tefillin* (phylacteries), may be called to read from the Torah, and may be counted as part of a *minyan,* the quorum of ten men required for a prayer service.

Sadly, this tremendous coming-of-age ritual, coinciding with the turbulent onset of adolescence, has been wrongly labeled either a tiresome chore or an excuse to party, rather than a moment of spiritual liberation. "It doesn't matter what happens in the Temple, it's the party that counts!" That's the view of Adam in *Keeping Up with the Steins.* It is a sentiment that could be echoed by Jews everywhere today. However, the message should be that it's the *mitzvah* that is the cause of the party, and not the other way around. Of course, welcoming a child into adulthood as a full and responsible member of the Jewish community deserves to be celebrated. The big irony is that this lavish celebration often marks the end and sum total of the boy's participation in his faith, not the beginning.

As we saw in the previous chapter, American Jews swiftly ascended into the middle class after World War II. Industrious and hardworking, they desperately wanted to leave behind the small businesses run by their parents' immigrant generation back in the Lower East Side. Going to a top college became the norm (as it had been before quotas were instituted in the 1910s), and soon Jews began holding previously unattainable positions as presidents of universities and at WASPy blue chip corporations. Jews eventually became among the most affluent of all ethnic minorities in the United States. History professor Edward S. Shapiro notes how the rapid economic and social mobility of Jews since WWII enabled them to leave the city slums and ghettos, and completely change the face of Jewish occupations in the United States within a few generations.[18] In a 2003 study, sociologist Lisa A. Keister used the National Longitudinal Survey of Youth to analyze the possible effects of religion on wealth in the United States.[19] The study showed that while Jews make up only 2 percent of the population in America, their median net worth is $150,890—more than three times the median of the entire sample ($48,200).[20]

By the 1950s and 1960s, anti-Semitic demagogues like Father Charles Coughlin were becoming a distant memory, while bigoted practices like the college quotas and running "restricted" clubs and hotels were declared illegal. American Jews wanted to show off their success and win the respect of a society that until recently had been openly hostile to them. So imagine the faces of *bubbes* and *zaydes* looking at the mountains of chopped liver at their grandson's bar mitzvah, as they recall childhoods when they could barely afford food. In its own way, all that excess represents a way of living the American Dream.

In his 2006 book about Jewish passivity and self-loathing, *The Wicked Son,* Pulitzer Prize–winning playwright David Mamet cynically notes in a chapter provocatively titled "Bar Mitzvah and Golden Calf" how after WWII the bar mitzvah became a euphemism for "conspicuous and bizarre consumption—a celebration of the wealth of the participants."[21] But a bar mitzvah should really be a family celebration that eases our young people into a new era of spiritual growth that has nothing to do with puppies in prayer shawls or being serenaded by Grammy-winning stars. Sure enough, the movie *Keeping Up with the Steins* ends with Benjamin convincing his family (much to his father's initial dismay) that an over-the-top party is just not for him. Instead, he holds a simple affair in the backyard, with entertainment provided by a klezmer band. The homemade lunch includes his relatives' favorite recipes instead of the tacky, overpriced baseball-themed food his father had had his heart set on.

At the end, Jewish pop music legend Neil Diamond shows up to sing "Hava Nagilah"—but not to infuse the party with the requisite celebrity appeal. Rather, Neil is a friend of Benjamin's grandmother, and she simply asked him to come. It's all a nod to the growing real-life backlash against Jewish mega celebrations, where some families are leaving the tuxes on the hangers and taking a meaningful trip to Israel or taking part in a social action project instead.

By the way, Diamond's cameo is also a knowing wink to that great pop culture myth of Jewish American assimilation—*The Jazz Singer.* Recall Krusty's father's throwaway line, "A jazz singer, this I could forgive. But a clown?" The story of the young, gifted Jewish singer who chooses fame as an entertainer over that of an obscure synagogue cantor (and breaks his parents' hearts) has resonated with American Jews since the original 1927 film.[22] The universally panned 1980 remake starred Neil Diamond in the role originated by the legendary Al Jolson (aka Asa Yoelson) and revealed the distance American Jews had traveled since the first film's début.[23] Diamond and his disappointed father, predictably overplayed by Sir Laurence Olivier, move about in a decidedly more glossy milieu than Jolson's gritty Lower East Side. The film's big finale sees the hugely successful Diamond on stage, with a blue scarf that resembles nothing so much as a prayer shawl draped around his neck. Diamond belts out the unforgettable anthem "America," a paean to immigrants who made the United States great. In spite of bad reviews (or maybe because of them) this campy remake has become a guilty viewing pleasure for many Jews, as Diamond's knowing cameo in *Keeping Up with the Steins* over twenty-five years later clearly indicates. Seeing Diamond, that icon of assimilation who even recorded a couple of Christmas albums in his time, serenading the bar mitzvah boy, is like watching the prodigal jazz singer coming home.

In an interesting postscript to *Keeping Up with the Steins,* its young star Daryl Sabara celebrated his own bar mitzvah just months after shooting wrapped on the film, and he's also attended some real-life bar mitzvahpaloozas. "I just sit back and laugh," says Sabara. "I know who they're about: The parents."[24] Had the movie taught him a lesson? "I already had a sense that it wasn't just about the party. After the movie, I didn't have any second thoughts."[25]

Daryl and his twin brother Evan Sabara had a joint bar mitzvah at the West Coast Chabad-Lubavitch headquarters. One unusual touch were table centerpieces with bundles of paperback books. The brothers explained that these titles, which ranged from *Tom Sawyer* to *Fahrenheit 451,* would be donated to their school; the books had been selected because they fit the curriculum's core reading requirements.[26]

The Sabaras' refreshing attitude marks a nice change from the shallow materialism we've been talking about.

Now that's what I call *nachas!*

" 3 "
BEYOND BUBBE:
THE 21ST-CENTURY JEWISH FAMILY

"The success of *Meet the Fockers* shows that America is familiar and comfortable enough with Judaism to get the jokes. Al Jazeera may be right."
—*Joel Stein*, Los Angeles Times[1]

n 2004, the movie *Meet the Fockers* (the sequel to 2000's *Meet the Parents*) raked in a staggering amount of gelt: half a billion dollars worldwide.[2] Now that's a lot of Jew gold!

Ben Stiller plays the unfortunately named Gaylord "Greg" Focker, a *nebbishy* male nurse who is engaged to Pam Danner (Teri Polo), the blonde, beautiful, bland, non-Jewish daughter of conservative WASP parents Jack and Dina Byrnes (Robert De Niro and Blythe Danner). Greg travels with Pam and the Byrnes to Miami to introduce them to his Jewish liberal parents, Roz and Bernie Focker (the Jewish dream team Barbra Streisand and Dustin Hoffman).

At the risk of attributing grand themes where none exist, *Meet the Fockers* does seem to be about "reverse assimilation," with most of the comedy arising out of the spectacle of laidback Jewish liberals teaching the conservative WASPs not to be so uptight. At the end of the movie, Mrs. Byrnes adopts a New York accent and picks up Yiddishisms from Roz, while Bernie declares Mr. Byrnes has been "Fockerized."

The Fockers are a hip and happy Jewish family. Greg's dad Bernie has built a "Wall of Gaylord" to honor his son's mediocre "accomplishments," which displays, along with his "Participant" trophies, Greg's framed bar mitzvah *talit* and *yarmulke*. It is telling that this symbol of a Jewish boy's elevation to manhood and religious responsibilities is kept behind glass, like a museum artifact. Streisand's Jewish mother is low-key but still stereotypical, slipping the occasional Yiddish word into her overbearing comments. Oh, and their dog is named "Moses."

The Fockers may be pretty hip, but in some ways they're also a throwback to stereotypical less-than-flattering portraits of Jewish families in comedies past.

Let's take a look at how the Jewish family in comedy has evolved from the twentieth century up to today:

1. INTERMARRIAGE

The Focker family dynamic is a familiar one. From the hit play Abie's Irish Rose (1928)[3] to TV's *Bridget Loves Bernie* (1972–1973)[4] and *Mad About You* (1992–1999),[5] Jewish intermarriage has been a staple of American comedy, even when it wasn't mentioned, as in the case of stand-up comedy legends George Burns and Gracie Allen. And by the twenty-first century, even the rabbi marries out of the faith. In *Keeping the Faith* (2000), Ben Stiller plays that very rabbi.[6] Rabbi Schram is caught in a love triangle over an Irish Catholic childhood pal, Anna (Jenna Elfman), with his best childhood friend, a Catholic priest played by Ed Norton. As if there could be any other outcome under the circumstances, the rabbi gets the girl, who then decides to convert to Judaism.

Stiller returned as Reuben Feffer in *Along Came Polly* (2004), playing an uptight, obsessive, *nebbish* Jew who this time marries a Jewish girl.[7] But before you can say "*mazel tov*," his new bride cheats while on their honeymoon. Stiller then finds love with the spontaneous, pretty, non-Jewish Polly (Jennifer Aniston). If the plot sounds familiar, it may be because Neil Simon's 1972 movie *The Heartbreak Kid* also featured a troubled, honeymooning Jewish couple.[8] That film was remade in 2007, starring—you guessed it—Ben Stiller.[9]

In the 2007 hit comedy *Knocked Up*, Ben Stone (Seth Rogen) is a proud Jew, complete with a stylish postmodern Jewfro and a passion for Stephen Spielberg's *Munich*: "In every movie with Jews, we're the ones getting killed," he explains. "*Munich* flips it on its ears."[10] He falls for lovely blonde non-Jewish Alison Scott (Katherine Heigl), and their unlikely relationship sets the stage for tasteless jokes—and moments of surprising tenderness.

In the quirky Oscar-winning 2007 comedy *Juno*, the titular heroine is impregnated by the nerdy character Bleeker ("I didn't think he had it in him," muses Juno's father).[11] Bleeker's Jewish identity is hinted at by the Hebrew alphabet chart seen hanging in his bedroom. Juno was directed by Jason Reitman, son of successful comedy director/producer Ivan (*Ghostbusters, Stripes, Animal House*).

The rare exceptions merely prove the rule. Her unlikely given name aside, Grace Adler (Debra Messing) of TV's *Will & Grace* was definitely Jewish, complete with a Brandeis degree. She was also beautiful, smart, funny—and she ends up married (for a short while) to a handsome Jewish doctor![12]

For many Jews, the funny side of intermarriage could be summed up in the title of Steve Solomon's 2006 one-man play "My Mother's Italian, My Father's Jewish, and I'm in Therapy!" Yet for others, marrying out of the faith is no laughing matter, and these comedies reflect a serious reality as intermarriage represents a direct threat to the very continuity of the Jewish people. In his 1994 book *Will We Have Jewish Grandchildren? Jewish Continuity and How to Achieve It,* chief rabbi of the British Commonwealth Sir Jonathan Sacks documents the rampant intermarriage taking place in America today noting, "For three generations—Jewish immigrants and their children and grandchildren—Jewish identity can be sustained. In the fourth generation, ties of kinship and ethnicity weaken and mixed marriage soars."[13]

Sacks notes that the intermarriage rate in the 1920s was "no more than 1 percent." Compare this to today when intermarriage rate hovers around 50 percent.[14]

And it is far higher among Jewish men, resulting in a crisis for Jewish women seeking that Jewish doctor or dentist of their dreams. The outlandish and offensive portrayal of Jewish women in contemporary comedy doesn't help. In *Keeping the Faith,* Jacob Schram, a hipster rabbi in a leather jacket, is introduced to a number of Jewish girls (he's considered the catch of the *Kiddush*), but these Jewish women are portrayed as desperate and unattractive.

Nowhere is this dichotomy between an "unattractive" Jewish woman and an exotic *shiksa* goddess more apparent than in *Curb Your Enthusiasm*. Larry's wife Cheryl is the non-Jewish trophy wife par excellence: beautiful, blonde, chic and supportive. "Oh boy, look at the Jew girl!" Larry exclaims while Cheryl cooks Passover dinner.[15] Meanwhile, Susie, the Jewish wife of Larry's agent and best friend, is sharp-tongued and frumpy despite (or perhaps because of) her garish designer ensembles.

You'd think Larry would be happy—that is, assuming you've never watched the show. In fact, Larry and Cheryl clash with some regularity. In the very first episode, Larry calls his wife "Hitler" in front of his manager's Jewish refugee parents.[16] By Season 6, Larry's lousy relationship skills finally drive his wife out of his life. When Cheryl calls him from a plane during a storm, fearing for her life, Larry is too busy with the TiVo guy to talk to her.[17] (This story line paralleled Larry David's very unfunny real-life split with his Jewish wife Laurie David.)

It's a more realistic portrayal of intermarriage than the one on display in *Meet the Fockers,* which glossed over conflicts between the couple by concentrating on clashes between the in-laws. *Curb*'s portrayal is more honest, breaking the previous "false and glossy veneer of Jewish-Gentile harmony (and the absence of brassy Jewish women) that otherwise has been *de rigueur* in contemporary prime-time sitcoms," notes an essay from the book *You Should See Yourself: Jewish Identity in Postmodern American Culture.*[18]

Interfaith catastrophes abound on *Curb*. Larry's ignorance of Christian custom creates havoc in the episode "Mary, Joseph and Larry." When Cheryl's parents ask what Larry is buying her for Christmas, he wryly responds, "my grandfather's tallis." Later Larry eats parts of a cookie nativity scene his in-laws have baked. "You ate the baby Jesus!" Cheryl's sister screams, as Larry replies, "I thought they were animal cookies."[19]

Larry's attitude to his own parents is far more sensitive. In "The Christ Nail," Cheryl's father takes to wearing a prop crucifixion nail from the movie *The Passion of the Christ* around his neck. Meanwhile, Larry needs to affix a *mezuzah* on his door before his father arrives (in a brilliant casting coup, Larry's father is played by old-time Jewish comic Shelley Berman); when he's desperate for a nail, guess what he commandeers while his father-in-law is asleep?[20]

The Torah commandment of Kibud Av va-Em is also the fifth of the Ten Commandments: "Honor your father and your mother as the Lord your God has commanded you." (Deuteronomy 5:16). The commandment seems self-evident, but as the sages note, it is one of the most difficult to keep. (Note that there's no corresponding commandment to honor your children!)

2. BUBBE (THE JEWISH MOTHER)

In 2007 alone, four books appeared, dedicated to revealing, analyzing and (sometimes) celebrating mom's every *kvetch*: from Laurie Rozakis' *The Portable Jewish Mother: Guilt, Food, and When Are You Giving Me Grandchildren?*[21] to Joyce Antler's *You Never Call! You Never Write!: A History of the Jewish Mother,*[22] Marnie Winston-Macauley's *Yiddishe Mamas: The Truth About the Jewish Mother*[23] to Judy *Gold's 25 Questions for a Jewish Mother*[24].

All these books explore and undermine the stereotypical Jewish mother: overbearing, emotionally stifling, sometimes hysterical, yet craftily intelligent, compulsively hardworking, and rarely out of mother mode.

What brought that on? It's been over a half century since TV pioneer Gertrude Berg played the beloved Jewish *shtetl bubbe* Molly on the comedy series *The Goldbergs*.[2] All but forgotten now, producer-writer-actress Berg was a pre-Lucy, pre-Oprah millionaire media maven. *The Goldbergs* were heard on radio from 1929 to 1946, and moved to the new medium of TV way back in 1949. And every show was live. Other spin-offs included a "Goldbergs" Broadway play and a comic strip.

The character of Molly Goldberg is the quintessential "Yiddishe Momme," the nourishing Old-World-Earth-Mother celebrated in sentimental vaudeville songs like "Jewish mother." The bedrock of the home, she's neither devastatingly beautiful nor terribly sophisticated, but a loyal survivor who guards her family like a lioness. Her entire existence was the pursuit of *nachas fun kinder* (joy from her children). Big-boned and even bigger-hearted, Molly is a lovingly meddlesome matriarch. Her honest portrayal of Jewish tenement life—trying to balance assimilation with tradition—resonated with Gentile and Jewish audiences alike.

America, for all its faults, is miles away from the *shtetls* of the Old Country, but that was hard for many Jewish matriarchs to accept. As Marnie Winston-Macauley notes in her book, *Yiddishe Mamas: The Truth About the Jewish Mother*, "when these women came to America[...] the very traits that meant survival in the *shtetl* community were seen as neurotic," especially by youngsters desperate to fit in with the culture at large, one that valued freedom and independence over family ties.[26]

"Disharmony between mother and child developed rather suddenly," writes Winston-Macauley, "and pain was the result, which provides fodder for both humor—and shrinks."[27] "Oedipus shmoedipus!" goes the old Freudian joke, "As long as he loves his mother."

And so the guilt-tripping, blousy, timid yet bossy Jewish mother became a world-famous archetype, thanks in large part to her children: the Philip Roths and Lenny Bruces and Woody Allens and countless other (mostly male) humorists who helped introduce her to American culture. Unlike the lovable Molly Goldberg, these portrayals were almost uniformly negative. In his classic book, *Portnoy's Complaint* (1969), Roth writes ruefully: "A Jewish man with parents alive is a fifteen-year-old boy and will remain a fifteen-year-old boy until the day he (or his parents) dies."[28]

As Jews moved up the class structure, the *shtetl bubbe* no longer had to work as hard. Later, the success of her husband and children might mean she didn't have to work at all. Why do all the *schlepping* when a *goy* can do it for her? Today, the character has morphed into a high-maintenance, menopausal mama, consumed with consuming, devoted to eating or shopping—or both at the same time. On *Saturday Night Live*, the *verklempt* Linda Richman (played by Mike Myers and named after his own Jewish mother-in-law) had time to host her very own TV show![29]

Another fictional example of this assimilated *shtetl bubbe* is the character of Sylvia Fine (Renee Taylor) on the 1990's sitcom *The Nanny*.[30] Brassy Sylvia, who loves food and tacky fashions, is determined to match her daughter (Fran Drescher) up with her rich Gentile boss, Mr. Sheffield; his religion doesn't interest her as much as his wallet does.

More recently, we have *South Park*'s Sheila Broflovski: a dowdy, heavy-set lady with a thick Brooklyn accent, married to the red yarmulke-wearing Gerald—pretty weird for residents of Colorado. Sheila figures prominently in an episode entitled "A South Park Christmas," where she puts her own spin on the Dreidel Song:

> *When you learn, to make the dreidel spin...*
> *You'll know, our people always win!* [31]

(PS: Sheila and Gerald are the first names of *South Park* Jewish cocreator Matt Stone's mother and father.)

Even action heroes have *shtetl* mamas. The heavily accented, nagging mother of *The Hebrew Hammer* (2003) dotes on her incontinent, diaper-wearing cat, but is distinctly unimpressed by her son's exciting crime-fighting career, even though he's a stereotype-busting, *tuchas*-kicking, proud Jewish boy who's just "saved Chanukah."

"It's not like it's a High Holy day..." his mother tuts.[32] In a brief exchange that sums up a half century of Jewish mama jokes, mother and son have a sweet little chat:

> *Mrs. Carver:* So, what are your plans for after the wedding?
>
> *Mordechai Jefferson Carver* (aka Hebrew Hammer): (*mutters*) Kill you.

Today, the Jewish mother character has become so "assimilated" that sometimes she is not even Jewish. Just think of the Mediterranean mamas in everything from *Moonstruck* (1987)[33] to *My Big Fat Greek Wedding* (2002).[34] Jewish actress Doris Roberts played a sort of *shiksa bubbe* on the long-running sitcom *Everybody Loves Raymond*— an overbearing busybody whose life revolves around cooking, cleaning and terrorizing her daughter-in-law.[35] (Surprise: Raymond's Italian-American TV family was co-created by executive producer Philip Rosenthal. On-screen Italian and other ethnic mothers often mirror their Jewish counterparts, indicating that the particularly "Jewish" aspects of the stereotype may not be as ethnically specific as one may think.)

In fact, as Joyce Antler explains in *You Never Call! You Never Write: A History of the Jewish Mother* (2007), our cell phone "umbilical cords" and hovering, so-called helicopter child-rearing styles mean we're all Jewish mothers now: "In the sense that today's parents are deeply, and perhaps inappropriately, involved in all manner of their children's daily lives, even those of adolescents and older children, the anxious modern middle-class parent may be said to resemble caricatures—if not of real-life Jewish mothers—of the past."[36]

So: how do these Jewish children turn out?

3. JEWISH AMERICAN PRINCESS

Self-absorbed, high-maintenance, whiny and materialistic—that's the stereotype of the Jewish American Princess, otherwise known as the "JAP." With Long Island as her ancestral homeland, the JAP is the Jewish mother's pampered offspring, literally her warm, nurturing *bubbe*'s polar opposite.[37]

Herman Wouk's best-selling novel *Marjorie Morningstar* popularized the stereotype of the Jewish American Princess back in 1955.[38] Marjorie, nee Morgenstern, is a spoiled, beautiful career girl from Central Park West who "manipulates men, has no talent, and is only interested in expensive clothing."[39] Next came Brenda Patimkin of Philip Roth's 1959 comic novella, *Goodbye, Columbus*[40]; note her surname, which sounds like "potemkin," the infamous Soviet painted façade without substance.

For reasons not entirely clear—increased acceptance? changing standards of beauty?—the pop culture image of the single, young Jewish female has evolved. For most of the twentieth century, she was caricatured as homely, awkward and needy: Comic vaudeville singer Sophie Tucker, who sang "Nobody Loves a Fat Girl, But Oh How a Fat Girl Can Love," and her "descendants" Joan Rivers, Bette Midler and Totie Fields; Gail Parent's 1972 novel *Sheila Levine Is Dead and Living in New York*[41]; Gilda Radner's "Jewess Jeans" girl on *Saturday Night Live*.[42]

Today, young Jewish women are often portrayed as poised and attractive. Not to mention blonde. When gorgeous, spoiled Goldie Hawn accidentally joins the army in the smash hit *Private Benjamin* (1980) she innocently asks an unsympathetic drill sergeant, "Excuse me, sir, is green the only color these [uniforms] come in?"[43] Her contemporary counterpart is the glamorous (and very ditzy) Cher Horowitz in the 1995 comedy *Clueless*.[44] Isabel Rose's 2005 novel turned musical *The JAP Chronicles* explores this transition in the person of the main character, Ali Cohen, an ugly duckling turned swan who seeks revenge on her former tormenters.[45]

The word "JAP" itself is also evolving, from the vicious putdown popular on 1980s college campuses (where you'd encounter anti-JAP graffiti, "Biggest JAP on Campus" contests, and housing ads that warned "No JAPs") to one "reclaimed" by female performers like Cathy Ladman, Jessica Kirson, Jackie Hoffman and Cory Kahaney, of 2007's stage smash "The JAP Show."[46]

No one personifies this transformation like the outrageous stand-up comedienne Sarah Silverman. Aptly described by Slate.com as a "JAP minstrel,"[47] Silverman "looks like someone you'd see at High Holiday services dressed in a very good copy of a Chanel suit with a couple of well-behaved toddlers by her side."[48] But Silverman's gimmick plays up the dichotomy between her innocent cuteness and all the ethnic slurs, self-absorbed observations and potty jokes delivered with a wide-eyed grin. One of the few printable bits from her 2007 *Sarah Silverman Program* on Comedy Central illustrates her annoying JAP-itude: "I can't even imagine what it would be like to be homeless. High school is the closest thing I can imagine to that. Y'know, 'cause it's cliquey…" [49]

As we've already noted, in movies, fiction and TV comedies, the bossy, unappealing Jewish girl is often contrasted unfavorably with the serene blonde "*shiksa* goddess," supposedly the idealized object of desire for ambitious Jewish men (like the upwardly mobile anti-heroes of Mordecai Richler and Philip Roth). In *Annie Hall* (1977),[50] Woody Allen's character plays up the difference between his first two wives, both Jewish, and his new uber-WASP girlfriend Diane Keaton, who "looks like the wife of an astronaut." Compared to Gentile trophy wives, Jewish girls are often portrayed as a kind of consolation prize.

More recently, the long-running, off-Broadway play *Jewtopia* (2004–2007) illustrates the staying power of these stereotypes decades after they'd become cliché.[51] The story revolves around two young men, a Jew (Adam Lipschitz) and a Gentile (Chris O'Connell), who, for dubious reasons, want to date their ethnic opposites: Chris thinks a Jewish girl will run his life and relieve him of taking responsibility, while Adam feels a *shiksa* will help him forget his ethnic background.

4. MY SON, THE *NEBBISH*

Indelibly personified by Woody Allen back in the 1960s, this male Jewish stereotype still makes appearances in movies and TV shows, as we've seen in our discussion of Larry David and in our brief overview of Ben Stiller's recent films. (In *Along Came Polly*, insurance analyst Stiller explains, "It's my job to worry").

The twenty-first-century iteration of the Jewish male retains traces of *nebbishness*, but also displays an edgy attitude reminiscent of Richard Dreyfuss's scruffy, hyper, cocky Jewish characters in *The Apprenticeship of Duddy Kravitz* (1974),[52] *Jaws* (1975),[53] and *The Goodbye Girl* (1977).[54] Seth Rogan, Paul Rudd, Jason Segel and Jonah Hill are a few of the stars in Jewish director Judd Apatow's constellation who seem to be channeling Dreyfuss's satirical outlook and boundless energy in movies like *The 40-Year-Old-Virgin* (2005),[55] *Knocked Up* (2007)[56] and *Superbad* (2007).[57]

The Hebrew Hammer (2003), starring Adam Goldberg, paved the way for a new kind of swaggering Jewish hero on film. He's sexy because he's Jewish, not in spite of it. The movie plays with African American and Jewish cultural touchstones: The Hammer drives a pimped-out white Cadillac with Magen David headlights; his license plate reads "l'chaim" and his fuzzy dice are really dreidels. After saving some Jewish children from older Christian bullies, he tells them solemnly, "Stay Jewish." The movie takes stereotypes about money and guilt and reveals their absurdity. The result is the first "Jewsploitation" film, one that's helped usher in a whole new comedy genre. In *Hot Rod* (2007),[58] Andy Samberg stars as an Evel Knievel–inspired stuntman—not exactly a profession commonly chosen by Jews. Meanwhile, superstar Adam Sandler is the brains behind *You Don't Mess with the Zohan* (2008)[59] about a former Mossad agent who dreams of becoming…a hairdresser.

It comes as no surprise that Jewish families have provided humorists with so much terrific material. Judaism has always been distinguished by its strong family life.

From the very outset, Judaism predicated its survival on family. The first commandment in the Torah is not about faith or belief, but rather to have children: "Be fruitful and multiply, and fill up the land" (Genesis 1:28). And Abraham is empowered by God to become the father of the Jewish people, not on account of his military strength or his righteousness but because "he will instruct his children and his household after him" (Genesis 18:19).

The home's central role in Jewish life ensured a safe haven of holy space during the Diaspora. Sadly, though, much modern comedy undermines the Jewish family rather than building it up. Humorists seem intent on biting the hand that fed them chicken soup. It's now a major put-down to be told you are "behaving like a Jewish mother," when it should be the biggest compliment you can give.

All-Jewish families have become a rarity in film and tv comedy—happy families, at least. The series *Arrested Development* (2003–2006),[60] created by Mitchell Hurwitz, depicts a dysfunctional Jewish family that makes *Curb Your Enthusiasm* seem like a *haftorah* reading. Yet the fact that Jews feel comfortable producing a show that makes them look so unsavory simply proves how far they have come in Hollywood, and in America.

Could the shortage of all-Jewish families on film, happy or otherwise, be because Jewish comedy writers themselves are often intermarried? They invented the JAP and the Jewish mother stereotypes in the fifties and sixties; maybe today's comics are still just "writing what they know." On the prime-time teenage soap opera *The OC* (created by the Jewish Josh Schwartz), the show's heartthrob lead has a Jewish father and a Protestant mother. As a way to merge the two faiths, he creates "Chrismukkah,"[61] and the show's popularity helped this new-century fake "holiday" gain traction beyond the small screen. *Time* magazine listed "Chrismukkah" as one of the "buzz words of 2004."[62] A newer show, *Weeds*, has also used it in a story line.[63]

The fact is, happy families don't sell tickets. It's one of the oldest rules in theater: Conflict makes for both high drama and low comedy. To cite just one example, the conflict inherent in a "mixed marriage" provided *I Love Lucy* with a vital comedic undercurrent.

Yet, I would like to see some all-Jewish couples in film and on TV for a change, beyond Gerald and Sheila Broflovski on *South Park*. Anybody that thinks a Jewish husband and a Jewish wife is not cause for comedy has clearly never been to my house! Fewer stereotypes would be nice, too. Fortunately, these days not every Jewish movie character has to be a *nebbish* or a JAP, as we have seen.

The very first mention of humor in the Bible concerns a Jewish mother, after all. Matriarch Sarah, the proto-*shtetl bubbe* herself, is told that God will bless her with her very first child—at the ripe old age of ninety-nine. She laughs, and who can blame her? But God is not amused: "Why did Sarah laugh? Is there something God cannot do?" (Genesis 18: 13–14).

When the child is born, Abraham and Sarah name the boy Isaac; the Hebrew "Yitzchak" comes from the root word "tzchok," meaning "laughter." Why? Because, as Sarah explains, "God has caused laughter to me." (Genesis 21: 6).

Given laughter's distinguished, even holy, pedigree, surely the time has come to stop laughing at Jewish women and the Jewish family and start laughing with them.

"4"

FAKE NEWS, REAL IMPACT

Reporter: "Let's say, hypothetically, I've got a friend, and he's an ambassador to a country called Fisrael: He's having a bit of trouble with an enemy in Iroon. Should he use his nuclear weapons against Iroon?"

Ambassador Gillerman: "Israel has never said that it has nuclear weapons."

Reporter: "No, no. Fisrael—Fisrael. Does Fisrael have nuclear weapons?"

Ambassador Gillerman: "Well I think you'll have to ask the Fisraeli ambassador."[1]

For Israeli ambassador to the UN Dan Gillerman, it must have been the craziest interview of his career. But for the folks behind *The Daily Show with Jon Stewart,* that exchange was just another clip for their vaults.

Since 1996, the Emmy and Peabody award-winning fake news broadcast has welcomed illustrious statesmen and newsmakers as guests, all of them evidently eager to shore up their "street cred" with the "kids."

Like satirical news shows of times gone by, from the BBC's *That Was the Week That Was*[2] and *Not the Nine O'Clock News*[3] to *Saturday Night Live*'s "Weekend Update," *The Daily Show* borrows the all-too-familiar trappings of a real broadcast: the portentous music, the slick sets, the anchor behind the desk complete with that little square above his shoulder that flashes illustrative graphics. But unlike those older programs, *The Daily Show* is often embraced by the very public figures it mocks. Moreover, *The Daily Show* isn't just considered entertainment. Incredibly, it's become a more-or-less legitimate news source for hundreds of thousands of viewers, and the biggest example of the latest trends in Jewish political humor.

Unlike their parents and grandparents, today's restless generation doesn't dutifully watch the news at 6:30 every night on one of the old Big Three networks. Instead, they can watch *The Daily Show* (often in groups in college dorms) when it airs or whenever they like, thanks to TiVo. A writing staff made up largely of Jewish Ivy League grads means *The Daily Show* comes across as written especially by and for hip, young people with a penchant for irony and iconoclasm. Jon Stewart acknowledged as much when he accepted his Emmy in 2005: "When I first said that I wanted us to put together a late-night comedy writing team that would only be 80 percent Ivy League–educated Jews, people thought I was crazy. They said you need 90, 95 percent. But we proved 'em wrong."[4]

While there is some utility in pointing out political ineptitude, there may also be some mistaken identity at play. In a March 2007 Pew Center report, people under thirty choose Jon Stewart and Bill O'Reilly as their favorite *journalists*.[5] The problem is, neither of them *are* journalists, they're commentators—one comedic, and the other comically angry. Young people are turning off the Dan Rathers, Wolf Blitzers and Anderson Coopers in exchange for jokes and righteous indignation masked as news, creating an audience gap between fake and real news. And in the ratings race, real news sources are losing. Don't think the newspaper and TV execs haven't noticed. For all their talk about "speaking truth to power" and "helping the community," news is a bottom-line industry like any other. Across America, news departments' budgets are getting slashed, which means they're doing fewer of those time- and money-consuming investigative reports that have been winning Emmys and Pulitzers since Watergate. Sure, Jon Stewart does some decent interviews, but there's only so much one can learn in seven minutes, especially when the interview is fake. Sarcasm can only supplement real journalism.

It's a vicious circle. Real news gets more and more shallow, *The Daily Show* mocks that shallowness and earns great ratings, so real news desperately responds with—still more slick, superficial "reportage." And so on. It's a little like cereal passing itself off as nutritional while it adds sugary goodness, which in turn drives some people toward sports nutrition bars packed with expensive calories. Sometimes we just need some oatmeal.

The fact remains that watching *The Daily Show* informs thousands of viewers who might otherwise remain completely ignorant of the day's complex, pressing (not to mention depressing) issues. Indeed, an April 2007 Pew Poll found that regular viewers of *The Daily Show* scored higher in tests of political knowledge than CNN viewers[6] (there's a lot of Pew Polls out there). After all, you can't make a "SCHIP" bill joke stick unless your audience already knows about the debate over taxpayer-funded children's health-care coverage, or refer repeatedly to "Mess O'Potamia" unless you assume your audience knows that Mesopotamia is the ancient name for what is now Iraq. No doubt, the program's humor is the sugar that helps the current affairs medicine go down.

Along with the satirical newspaper *The Onion*, *The Daily Show* blurs the line between fact and fiction, and offers analysis through satire of the inherent contradictions in both the news stories themselves and their presentation (just watch a real newscast during hurricane season, when hyperventilating reporters typically spew as much hot air as a tropical storm). It's a sign of the times when people running to catch a morning train can grab *The Onion* or *Metro* to read on the way to work. (Incidentally, *Daily Show* cocreator Ben Karlin cut his comedy chops while at the University of Wisconsin writing satire for the former.)

So what does fake news offer that real news doesn't or can't? Aside from an angry, generally left wing point of view, it's an outlet for millions of people who don't have a media platform of their own, who find themselves yelling at their TVs more often than not. *The Daily Show* hears those shouts and echoes them back in a funny, reassuring way. The program grapples with the inconsistencies and contradictions ignored by the mainstream media, and gives voice to our frustrations with traditional news. If you look past *The Daily Show*'s cynicism, you see a real attempt to introduce ideas into the nation's political conversation.

It's not like the news media hasn't set itself up for parody. The wall between news and entertainment began to erode after President Ronald Reagan deregulated the media in the early 1980s, and radio stations no longer had to have news departments to retain their broadcasting licenses. Meanwhile, newspapers and TV networks began shutting down expensive and often danger-rife foreign bureaus. When it comes to securing precious advertising dollars, amusement generally beats information, so news started chasing entertainment in order to compete.[7] The first Gulf War may have begun the trend, when CNN turned its coverage into a prime time drama, and the O. J. Simpson slow-speed chase of 1994 may have been the breaking point; news outlets found that O. J. was as good as the still-nascent reality television—the "story" wrote itself, no talent needed. And while all this was going on, today's college freshman was an impressionable child. No wonder Britney trumps Burma in the news ratings. No wonder Jon Stewart hosts the Oscars. Expect more of such overlap as the YouTube generation becomes the *main* demographic.

The strange result is that while traditional news adopts the trappings of entertainment and becomes less informative, certain spheres of comedy have adopted the trappings of informative news and created a new hybrid form of social analysis. If news media warped into info-tainment, some entertainment has become fact-tetiousness.[8]

The Daily Show's rise comes at a time when the way we receive and preserve information is changing dramatically. Consider the exponential growth of blogging, a phenomenon that encourages the idea that anybody can be a "real" journalist. The number of these DIY first-person Web sites has grown from approximately 1 million in 2003 to nearly 73 million in 2007.[9] While many blogs are simply embarrassingly intimate personal diaries, some practice "citizen journalism," actually breaking local news, like reporting Hurricane Katrina from the heart of New Orleans.

Meanwhile, viral sites like Facebook and YouTube make it easier than ever before to spread pro- and anti-Semitic messages around the world in seconds with the touch of a button. Comments on provocative blogs feature mostly misspelled vitriol, junk science, historical revisionism and urban legends, all in all generating far more heat than light. In its own weird way, all this "Karaoke journalism" is democratizing society. A site like RateMyProfessor.com turns the traditional teacher/student relationship on its head. Users treat the site as a blackboard where students grade their teachers, rather than the other way around.

In short, we now have a greater breadth of news media, but far less depth. The ubiquitous stock market–inspired news tickers that flow across screens large and small—from big-screen plasmas to BlackBerries and iPhones—embody most people's idea of "news." The twenty-four-hour news cycle hurts fact-checking. Young people have little experience with the in-depth investigative reporting their parents once demanded the major networks and newspapers to deliver; such investigative reporting is increasingly rare, and decreasing attention spans combined with a proliferation of choice would make such reporting hard for younger viewers to digest in any event.

During the 2004 presidential elections, *The Daily Show*'s popularity and influence reached a peak. Jon Stewart became a political pundit in his own right, penning *America (The Book): A Citizen's Guide to Democracy Inaction*, which topped the best-seller lists.[10] In one memorable confrontation, conservative *Crossfire* panelist Tucker Carlson asked Stewart rather brusquely why he didn't ask Democratic candidate John Kerry "real questions" when Kerry appeared on *The Daily Show*. Stewart replied testily, "You're on CNN. The show that leads into me is puppets making crank phone calls."[11]

Yet at least one CNN big-wig seemed to take *The Daily Show* pretty seriously. Not long after Stewart accused Carlson and his CNN co-host Paul Begala of "partisan hackery" and begged them (jokingly) to "stop hurting America," CNN announced the cancellation of the long-running *Crossfire*. More recently, the frequently fired Tucker Carlson found himself "cancelled" yet again, while Stewart's ratings remain steady.

"I guess I come down more firmly in the Jon Stewart camp," explained CNN chief executive Jonathan Klein, who also said he would prefer to air more substantive, less aggressive discussion of current events on his network.[12] Stewart responded, "I had no idea that if you wanted a show canceled, all you had to do was say it out loud."[13]

It's also a great way to add a new word to the nation's vocabulary. In the pilot episode of the inevitable *Daily Show* spin-off, *The Colbert Report*, the show's fake conservative commentator Stephen Colbert used the word "truthiness" as a synonym for that gut feeling that something is so despite the evidence. The coined word caught on. "Truthiness" was named Word of the Year for 2005 by the American Dialect Society and for 2006 by Merriam-Webster.[14]

A bombastic, self-assured pundit in the Bill O'Reilly mode, Colbert and his on-screen persona are nominally Catholic, so Jewish jokes (written by a staff of mostly Jewish writers, naturally) often play up the character's earnest ignorance. During Yom Kippur, Colbert unveiled his special Atonement Hotline, a white rotary phone with a Star of David on it. Callers heard, "At the beep, please be a *mensch,* and unburden your soul by stating how you've wronged me—Stephen Colbert. Your call will not be returned but selected apologies will be played on the air. You should be so lucky."[15]

Both programs are peppered with similar Yiddishisms and Jewish jokes, lending them a one-of-a-kind "Borscht Belt Meets Ivy League" sensibility that accounts in large part for their popularity. In one particularly memorable episode of *The Daily Show,* the combination of "inside" Jewish humor and self-conscious, postmodern fakery reached an apex—the night Borat showed up. In other words, a fake anchorman interviewed a fake reporter about a fake documentary. When Stewart raised his coffee cup and offered the traditional Jewish toast, "l'chaim," Borat didn't understand what the word meant. When Stewart explained that it meant "to life," Borat misheard it as "to laugh"—"to laugh at the Jew." Stewart kept trying to explain, to which Borat responded "to life to us—death to the Jew!" When Stewart finally said that he himself is Jewish, Borat replied, "You have had, *eh,* plastic surgery, though you don't look like a Jew—you have—you have had—you have had your horns removed?"[16] The encounter was dramatically— or should that be comedically—different from those depicted in the movie *Borat,* in which Baron Cohen's interview subjects innocently play along with his absurd anti-Semitic assertions.

On *The Daily Show,* however, the audience is hip to the joke, and it's a safe one to make, in a nation where

Jewish people are by and large secure and successful. Yet the victimhood troupe retains its comedic power, which wouldn't be true if there weren't still a frisson of danger in simply being a Jew. This danger has inspired the paradoxical Jewish persona of the simultaneous insider/outsider, which gives them a valuable, unexpected perspective on what's going on around them.

Rob Kutner, one of the show's many Jewish writers, believes *The Daily Show*'s popularity reflects an environment in which Jews are more comfortable having fun with their identity, adding that the Jew's intrinsic outsider status is actually a plus in today's worrisome world:

"Jon, even though he isn't observant, feels comfortable relating openly to the fact that he is Jewish. It gives him an idiom, a frame of reference. In some way, I think he plays on the typical Jewish attributes: That we are outsiders, reflecting on the mainstream, and standing up to the establishment."[17]

Indeed, Jon Stewart (he was born Jonathan Stewart Leibowitz but changed his name because—get this nod to the whole history of American Jewish comedy—"it sounded too Hollywood") belongs to a long tradition of Jewish political satirists. In the satirically seminal sixties, Jewish stand-up comics Mort Sahl and Lenny Bruce based their biting, topical routines on the daily news.

"Will Rogers…came on the stage and impersonated a yokel who was critical of the federal government," Sahl once observed. "And when I come on the stage, I impersonate an intellectual who is critical of yokels who are running the government."[18]

Of course, Lenny Bruce's tumultuous life and early death are legendary today but Mort Sahl's contemporaneous career is mostly forgotten, except by comedy buffs and famous admirers like Albert Brooks: "Every comedian who is not doing wife jokes has to thank him for that," says Brooks. "He really was the first, even before Lenny Bruce, in terms of talking about stuff, not just doing punch lines."[19]

Contemporary comics who've taken on the mantle of Bruce and Sahl include *The Daily Show* regular Lewis Black, who has skewered both Democrats and Republicans. They also include former *Saturday Night Live* writer-turned-combative satirist and political candidate Al Franken, who has said, "The fact that Jews really revere comedy was part of the reason I chose it. Humor is respected in Jewish life. Even rabbis try to be funny."[21]

Just look at me.

There is something very Jewish about grappling with the discrepancies of power. Like Lewis Black once said, "You elected Bush, so that's who I'm going to rant about. If you elect Kerry, I'm going to rant about him, too. My problem is with authority!"[22]

Jews have a history of wrestling with higher authorities. The biblical patriarch Jacob famously wrestled with an angel and was given a new name from God for his troubles: "No more shall you be called Jacob, but Israel," declared the angel. "For you have wrestled with God and with men, and have prevailed" (Genesis 32:29).

And ever since, wrestling with God (and power) has been at the core of Jewish identity.

The voluminous Talmud dissects every aspect of Jewish law, belief, philosophy and tradition. It is more a book about arguments, than answers. In fact, many Talmudic questions never reach a suitable conclusion and end with the word taiku, meaning "the question stands." Throughout the Talmud, we read of one sage verbally wrestling with another to prove that the law agrees with his view. The Talmud is still taught this way today: The startling sight (and sound) of yeshiva scholars screaming at each other face-to-face is one to behold!

This argumentative style of questioning prompted the famous adage, "Two Jews, three opinions." Funnily enough, this saying is predated by a passage in the Talmud. Rebbi, the sage who taught that one should not laugh in this world, was asked, "If one has two heads, on which one should he place his *tefillin* (phylacteries)?" Surprisingly enough, the Talmud continues, "Meanwhile, a man came to the academy saying that he had just begotten a two-headed son and wanted to know how much must be given to the priest for the redemption of the first-born" (Talmud, Menachos 37a). Naturally, the commentators tease out the serious underpinnings to this seemingly absurd story.

As you can see, many debates in the Talmud take strange, wonderful segues with a humor all their own— some of which is intentional. For example, we read that Rabba, the eminent sage of his generation, began his classes with humorous observations (Talmud, Pesachim 117a). His purpose was not just to entertain, but also to open his students' minds and make them into eager receptacles for wisdom.

William Novak and Moshe Waldoks dedicate a chapter in their famous *Big Book of Jewish Humor* to the notion that Talmudic logic and process has imprinted itself upon Jewish humor: "Improbable logic, slightly convoluted arguments, skepticism, and a remarkable desire to equate intelligence with common sense—these are some of the characteristics of the rabbinic mind, as well as of Jewish humor."[23]

OK, it's not likely that Jon Stewart or his writers study Talmud between shows. But this tradition of intellectual inquiry has clearly filtered down to Jewish comedians, as has the habit of greeting adversity with bitter humor. Back in the "old country," Jewish humor critiqued the shortcomings and absurdities of Russian rulers, first the czar and then the Soviet government. In *Fiddler on the Roof,* the rabbi jokingly prays, "May God bless and keep the czar...far away from us."[24]

Today, Jon Stewart, like the great sage Rabba, uses humor to make his piercing satire more palatable to audiences—and help them cope with an increasingly crazy world.

But can humor do something more? Can comedy actually make the world a better place?

On rare occasions, satire takes a holiday on *The Daily Show.* When it returned to the air after 9/11, the show's introduction included footage of the attack. Then a tearful Stewart discussed his personal view on the event for nine minutes, dropping the anchorman pose and coming across more like the college kid's very own Commander in Chief. He concluded powerfully: "The view from my apartment...was the World Trade Center...and now it's gone. And they attacked it, this symbol of American ingenuity, and strength, and...and labor, and imagination and commerce, and it is gone. But you know what the view is now? The Statue of Liberty. The view from the South of Manhattan is now the Statue of Liberty. You can't beat that."[25]

On September 11, it was assumed that people under forty were so coolly detached that they couldn't properly come to terms with the magnitude of the attack, and this detachment was chalked up to their lifelong diet of pop-culture irony. While Stewart's "serious moment" proved pundits wrong, in general *The Daily Show* actually takes advantage of its young audience's comfort with the ironic, helping them deal with events like 9/11 by speaking their language. Situations are taken to their logically absurd conclusions, and the audience emerges with a new recognition.

"Give any tragedy enough time," Lenny Bruce said, "and people will let you make fun of it." Post–9/11, a handful of comics are trying to offer a glimmer of hope through humor, however small. The Axis of Evil Comedy Tour, for example, features a trio of Middle Eastern stand-ups, while the Israeli Palestinian Comedy Tour brings together a motley quartet of Jewish and Muslim comedians.

On a somewhat grander scale, Jewish comedian Albert Brooks released his provocatively titled movie *Looking for Comedy in the Muslim World* in 2006.[26] The plot sees Brooks being hired by the U.S. State Department to discover what makes Muslims laugh. Promised a Medal of Freedom for his troubles ("the nice one" with "the colored ribbon"), Brooks heads off to…India, which despite its sizable Muslim population, is 80 percent Hindu. The movie's promising concept derails at that point, and becomes just another episodic fish out of water comedy, with Brooks seemingly afraid to pull out all the stops and confront humorless radical Islam.

Movie audiences turned out to be indifferent to

Brooks's good intentions. His idiosyncratic humor has always been an acquired taste, and this uneven effort was no exception. *Looking for Comedy in the Muslim World* had the potential to be humorously explosive, but it turned out to be a bomb of a different kind—it tanked at the box office.[27]

As the 2008 election approached, media watchers, politicos and cultural theorists were waiting to see how *The Daily Show* would handle Barack Obama and John McCain. Would the show's influence remains as great as it supposedly was in 2004—when, for all the program's wild popularity with that younger demographic, a Republican incumbent was reelected by a much larger and older voting block?

Can a fake newscaster influence an election? The idea was taken to its illogical conclusion in Barry Levinson's 2006 movie comedy *Man of the Year*, starring Robin Williams as a Stewart-esque political talk show host who, through a sequence of absurd events, becomes president of the United States.[28]

Life didn't imitate art the following year, though. Did Stephen Colbert's aborted "real" run for the presidency in 2008 indicate a populist protest killed off before it could build steam, a publicity stunt, or an empty, fashionable, narcissistic gesture? Maybe he would have chosen Stewart as his running mate. At least a Colbert/Stewart ticket would be authentically fake bipartisanship, which for many in a certain demographic might be a political step up.

"5" SERIOUSLY FUNNY:
ANTI-SEMITISM AND SELF-HATRED

"The Jews are responsible for all the wars in the world."[1]
—*Mel Gibson*

"I would like to meet the fearless anti-Jew warrior,
Melvin Gibson. We agree with his comments that the Jews
started all wars."[2]
—*Borat*

The hard-drinking crowd in the Tucson bar gives the stranger with the funny name a hootin', hollerin' welcome as he takes the stage. Decked out like a cowboy, Borat Sagdiyev—the visiting "reporter" from faraway Kazakhstan—wows 'em with a catchy ode to national freedom entitled "In My Country There Is Problem."

The tune starts innocently enough, then takes a disturbing turn:

> *In my country there is problem,*
> *And that problem is the Jew.*
> *They take everybody's money,*
> *They never give it back.*
> *Throw the Jew down the well,*
> *So my country can be free.*
> *You must grab him by his horns,*
> *Then we have big party.*[3]

This scene from the cult TV comedy *Da Ali G Show* was a slight departure for the hit show, in which a heavily disguised and apparently illiterate Sacha Baron Cohen (in reality a Cambridge-educated, Hebrew-speaking Kibbutz kid who played Tevye in a college production of *Fiddler on the Roof*) "interviewed" the famous and powerful, some of whom endured this excruciating experience with more aplomb (Newt Gingrich) than others (Donald Trump).

Baron Cohen's move to the big screen, with 2006's smash "mockumentary" film *Borat: Cultural Learnings of America for Make Benefit Glorious Nation of Kazakhstan,* focused the comedian's attention on ordinary people across America: rodeo crowds, a gun shop owner, the hosts of a bed and breakfast.[4] In the film, Baron Cohen's crass, dimwitted character travels "the U. S. and A." by ice cream van instead of by plane, in case "the Jews repeated their attack of 9/11." Movie audiences cringed and cracked up as their uncouth antihero lurched from one appalling misadventure to the next.

This outrageous, low-brow, politically incorrect film raked in the cash and became a cultural phenomenon, sparking tens of thousands of outraged or laudatory words. No doubt Baron Cohen knew he'd really made it big in twenty-first-century America when he and his film became the subject of a couple of lawsuits, not to mention an international incident: The Kazakhstan government felt obliged to take out a four-page ad in *The New York Times* challenging Cohen's unflattering depiction of their country as a filthy, backward *shetl,* and his character's summation of Kazakhstan's problems as "economic, social and Jew." Kazakh deputy foreign minister

Rakhat Aliyev probably didn't help his case by earnestly insisting that, in his country, "women not only travel inside buses but also their own cars," that "we make wine from grapes"—not, as Borat had insisted, fermented horse urine—"and Jews can freely attend synagogues."[5] Displaying more savvy and sophistication than his fellow countryman, Kazakhstan's ambassador to the UN acknowledged Baron Cohen's obvious comedic talent ("Some scenes really made me laugh"), adding: "Having survived Stalin, we will certainly survive Borat. But please understand why our laughter is selective."[6]

For those who loved the film, Borat offered a break from years of stifling "political correctness." Weary of being told what to say and how to say it, fans embraced Borat as their surrogate, a trickster immune from the consequences of his offensive antics. Borat is the anti-Latka; but unlike the lovable, naive foreigner embodied by Andy Kaufman on the TV series *Taxi*, Borat is crude and lewd—a life-sized Id in a tiny neon swimsuit. At the same time, the character's crude, clueless behavior, cheap suit, and cheesy 1970s mustache mark Borat as someone we're not supposed to want to be like.

Good thing, too, because *Borat* is loaded with shocking anti-Semitic scenes, from the "running of the Jew" event, in which Kazakh villagers club enormous "Jew" puppets with horns on their heads as part of an annual festival, to the scene in the gun shop:

Borat: "What kind of a gun would you recommend to kill a Jew?"

Gun dealer: "I'd recommend a 9-mm or a Glock automatic."

So why did this movie strike such a nerve? Timing, for one thing. Like all good comics, Baron Cohen tapped into the zeitgeist. It's no coincidence that *Borat* was released at a time in which, by any measure, the old scourge of anti-Semitism was on the rise again worldwide.

According to U.S. State Department Reports, anti-Semitism around the globe has increased significantly in recent years, with over half the reported incidents taking place in Western Europe—where a radical Muslim population has also increased.[7] Everything from verbal and physical assaults to attacks on Jewish property like schools and synagogues were said to be on the rise.

This "new anti-Semitism" appears to target Jews as a nation rather than as separate individuals, and is often cloaked in the language of anti-Zionism. Iran's supreme leader, Ayatollah Khamenei, calls Israel a "cancerous tumor of a state [that] should be removed from the region,"[8] and the nation's president, Mahmoud Ahmadinejad, has repeatedly called the Holocaust "a myth," even holding a Holocaust-denial conference—not a reassuring sign from a country that appears to be flexing its nuclear muscles.

Hitler's embittered, anti-Semitic autobiography *Mein Kampf* continues to sell briskly, while the notorious *Protocols of the Elders of Zion* was adapted into a notorious thirty-part 2002 mini-series for Egyptian TV and presented as historical fact.[9] Of course, as London reporter Philip Graves proved back in 1921, *Protocols* was a forgery cooked up by Russian intelligence at the behest of the czar, purportedly revealing plans by a secret (purely imaginary) Jewish cabal to take over the world.[10] Both works, long dismissed as patently stupid, evil relics of unenlightened times, have recently found millions of new readers via the Internet.

Compared to just about every other nation on Earth, America was and remains a haven for Jews, who flocked to its shores throughout the late nineteenth and early twentieth centuries, and for the most part found freedom, safety and prosperity. Yet even the United States isn't immune from the contagion of bigotry. The matter-of-fact anti-Semitism on display in *Borat* reflects the findings of Gabriel Schoenfeld in his 2004 book *The Return of Anti-Semitism*. He writes, "The passions roiling the Islamic world are hardly the end of the matter. For anti-Semitism has also reawakened dramatically in Europe, where it was long thought to be completely dormant, if not entirely extinct. And it is also making an unprecedented headway in new precincts in the United States, a country where it has never before found truly fertile soil."[11] For example, and no pun intended, in 2007 a New Jersey state police helicopter discovered a swastika about the size of a football field cut into a cornfield, like a racist crop circle.[12]

Many observers, such as Canada's former justice minister Irwin Cotler, warn that Jews face a "gathering storm" of bigotry, not seen since the rise of Nazi Germany in the 1930s. Pointing to outright threats coming from Hezbollah, al-Qaeda and Hamas, Cotler told the 2007 Conference on the Future of the Jewish People, "There's been a quantum leap forward in Iran acquiring lethal atomic capabilities and increased state support for international and Mideast terrorism. Iran not only continues to incite a Mideast Holocaust but now also denies that the European one occurred."[13] Many

Arab nations are increasingly bellicose when it comes to dealing with their Jewish neighbors.

Reacting to his Golden Globe nomination for *Borat,* Baron Cohen made a rare out-of-character statement: "I have been trying to let Borat know this great news, but for the last four hours both of Kazakhstan's telephones have been engaged. Eventually, Premier Nazarbayev answered and said he would pass on the message as soon as Borat returned from Iran, where he is guest of honor at the Holocaust Denial Conference."[14]

Is it any surprise that *Borat* was banned in every Arab nation except Lebanon?

In an interview with *Rolling Stone,* Baron Cohen explained the "minstrelsy" he employed in *Borat:* "By himself being anti-Semitic, [Borat] lets people lower their guard and expose their own prejudice."

He added, "When I was in university, there was this major historian of the Third Reich, Ian Kershaw, who said, 'The path to Auschwitz was paved with indifference.' I know it's not very funny, being a comedian talking about the Holocaust, but it's an interesting idea that not everyone in Germany had to be a raving anti-Semite. They just had to be apathetic."[15]

So the film's outrageous "anti-anti-Semitism"[16] (as the *New York Times'* Sharon Waxman described it) is Baron Cohen's way of fighting back. However, Robert Wistrich, head of the Center for the Study of Anti-Semitism at Israel's Hebrew University, worries that Baron Cohen's subtle reasoning will be lost on less nimble-minded viewers. "The purpose of this kind of comedy is to show how ridiculous prejudices and stereotypes are," writes Wistrich, "but using the stereotypes can actually perpetuate them."[17]

It's telling that so many Jewish comedians (and their audiences) have recently declared the Holocaust "on limits" for comedy, while as its horrors recede into the distant past, the macabre phenomenon of Holocaust denial is growing. Contentious works like (non-Jewish actor/director) Roberto Benigni's Oscar-winning movie *Life Is Beautiful* (1997)[18] and Art Spiegelman's graphic novel *Maus* (1991)[19] made the Holocaust an acceptable subject for less than reverent mediums of expression. In 2008, *National Lampoon* cartoonist Sam Gross released a book called *We Have Ways of Making You Laugh: 120 Funny Swastika Cartoons* (one depicts the serpent in the Garden of Eden telling Adam and Eve, who are wearing swastika armbands, "You ate something that made you stupid.")[20]

It goes without saying that this sort of gallows humor offends Holocaust survivors and their families. Has "Nazi" become the Jewish "N" word? Whether or not it's an acceptable punch line depends upon who's using it. And as a rabbi, much of this humor makes me deeply uncomfortable—it certainly isn't material for a Shabbat sermon.

As Annette Insdorf and others have pointed out, we run the risk of trivializing the horrors of the past, although it could be argued that making Nazi jokes is a healthy expression of self-confidence, and having the last laugh gives Jews the final victory over their enemies.[21]

Larry David has played a huge role in the mainstreaming of Holocaust jokes. David cowrote an unforgettable 1994 *Seinfeld* episode in which Jerry is caught making out during *Schindler's List.*[22] Then on *Curb Your Enthusiasm*, David takes the breaking of Holocaust taboos to a new level. Larry's rabbi asks if he can bring a friend "who's a survivor" to Larry and Cheryl's dinner party. So Larry invites his father's friend, Solly, who's a Holocaust survivor himself. But unlike Solly, the rabbi's friend never set foot in a concentration camp. It turns out that this tanned young hunk named Colby Donaldson was a star on the reality show *Survivor*.

Colby captivates the other dinner guests with his tales of battling snakes in the Australian outback, until finally, Solly can't take it any longer: "Let me tell you, I was in a concentration camp. You never even suffered one minute in your life compared to what I went through."

Incredibly, Colby actually defends himself: "I couldn't even work out over there. They certainly didn't even have a gym. I wore my sneakers out, and the next thing you know, I'm in my flip-flops."

The conversation devolves into a game of one-upmanship:

Colby: We had very little rations, no snacks.

Solly: Snacks? What are you talking, snacks? We didn't eat, sometimes for a week, for a month...

Colby: Have you even seen the show?

Solly: Did you ever see *our* show? It was called the Holocaust!

The scene ends with the two men yelling at each other, "I'm a survivor! I'm a survivor!"[23]

Like Colby, many Jews (and non-Jews) today equate "suffering" with a few weeks without sneakers, if they think about suffering at all. We've become so material-istic, so immune to true deprivation, that the latest low-jinks of teenaged starlets inspire bigger headlines than suicide bombings. Historical illiteracy is at a dangerous high, and our sense of proportion at an all-time low.

It's these attitudes that Sarah Silverman spoofs in her routine about the Holocaust: "My niece goes to Hebrew school. She called me the other day and was talking to me and said, 'Aunt Sarah, did you know that Adolf Hitler killed sixty million Jews?' And I told her, 'Hon-ey, I think it's actually six million.' And she said, 'Yeah, you're right. But really, what's the difference?' What's the difference! I mean, really! Sixty million would be unforgivable!'"[24]

Meanwhile, one of Sacha Baron Cohen's non-*Borat* per-sonas, the flamboyantly gay fashion stylist Bruno, blithely rates celebrity red-carpet looks as either "in the ghetto" (thumbs up) or "train to Auschwitz" (thumbs down).

Context and narrative point-of-view are everything, and are what separate an insightful gag that treads the line of taste from a tasteless joke. Larry David, Sacha Baron Cohen and Sarah Silverman all share offensive/ naïve stage personas, and those personas help escort the audience through a joke that reveals a larger point of view within a specific context. The "survivor" bit didn't just rely on a mix-up of terminology, but satirized the way we overvalue (fake) celebrity and undervalue (real) history. Sarah Silverman uses absurdity to remind us of the gravity of the Holocaust, not make fun of it. In one skit, she hands out cooking utensils and appliances to black passersby as an apology for 400 years of slavery: "I'm sorry for slavery—here's your toaster." Her naïve persona doesn't understand how offensively ineffectual the gesture is, but the audience should.[25] The legacy of slavery overwhelms our attempts to discuss it. By playing the character of a no-excuses bigot, Silverman forces her audiences to confront their own prejudices.

There's always a bit of lag between some historic tragedy and the comedy that later helps us contextualize and come to grips with it. Before very long, the terrorist attacks on America that occurred on September 11, 2001, in which nearly 3,000 people lost their lives, also lost its off-limits stigma—at least among the "shtick shift" comics working in a new climate of panic and uncertainty to try to offer consolation and commentary through humor.

On *Curb Your Enthusiasm,* Larry offends his rabbi by innocently saying "Let's roll!" (reportedly the rallying cry of a rebellious passenger on the doomed flight United 93). The rabbi explains that his brother died on 9/11 and Larry is chastened—until the rabbi explains that his brother was killed in Manhattan that day in an unrelated accident. Larry being Larry, can't help but respond sarcastically: "Oh, I didn't know, I didn't know that if you, that if you, you died *uptown* on 9/11 that it was, that it was part of it, uh…the tragedy!"[26]

In another episode, Larry hears a rumor that a terrorist attack is about to strike Los Angeles. His wife has made a very important charitable commitment and doesn't want to leave town—so he tells her he's going to leave without her, to go golfing:

Cheryl: Just seems like if we're gonna go, we should go together.

Larry: Well, not necessarily. Almost seems a little selfish that you would want both of us to… perish.

Cheryl: So, you'd be fine going on without me.

Larry: Well, it would be…very difficult at first, I'm sure. But hopefully at some point, I'd get back some semblance of a life.[27]

Humor has always been the way Jews have dealt with hardship and looming terror, going back to the book of Proverbs: "A joyful heart is good medicine, a broken spirit dries the bones" (17:22). Humor as a coping mechanism has aided Jews throughout the ages; Emil Fackenheim, a noted philosopher and survivor of Auschwitz, observed, "We kept our morale through humor."[28]

Harder to explain is the puzzling concept of the "self-hating Jew," one that's amused and intrigued many a modern Jewish humorist. When, on *Curb Your Enthusiasm*, a fellow Jew berates Larry David for whistling Wagner, calling him a self-hating Jew, David replies, "I do hate myself, but it has nothing to do with being Jewish."[29] It's become such a commonplace observation among Jewish comedians like Woody Allen ("I have frequently been accused of being a self-hating Jew, and while it's true I am Jewish and I don't like myself very much, it's not because of my persuasion."[30]) that even imaginary members of the tribe express the same sentiment; *The Simpsons* Krusty the Clown illustrated the very absurdity of the notion by taking it to its logical conclusion: "All this time I thought I was a self-hating Jew, and now I'm just an anti-Semite!"[31]

The rationale seems to be: If you beat your enemy to the punch line by getting in the first and last word, even if you lose, you still win. This idea was in full effect when in 2006 the Iranian newspaper *Hamshahri* held a Holocaust cartoon contest in response to the controversial Danish cartoons of the prophet Mohamed. In response to *that* response, two Israeli cartoonists, Amitai Sandy and Eyal Zusman, held their own anti-Semitic cartoon contest: "We'll show the world we can do the best, sharpest, most offensive Jew-hating cartoons ever published. No Iranian will beat us on our home turf."[32] Sandy reported that the response was 90 percent positive, and that the point of this exercise in free speech was not to laugh at Muslims. "We think a real demonstration would be to laugh at yourself, your own religion and values. I hope the Muslims who protested see our cartoons and then think twice before they accept anti-Semitic messages as the truth."[33]

And because Jewish comedians have been America's jesters of choice throughout the twentieth century (in 1979, *Time* estimated that 80 percent of the country's professional comedians were Jewish[34]), it's no wonder that an anxious nation turns to them to help make sense of a world turned upside down in the twenty-first century. How else can anyone process the bizarre conspiracy theories surrounding 9/11—that it was a Mossad plot, and that no Jews were killed in the attack—than by joking? In fact, in David Deutsch and Joshua Newman's 2005 book entitled *The Big Book of Jewish Conspiracies*, the authors do exactly that, giving a range of humorous takes on Jewish conspiracy theories, including 9/11.[35]

The specter of anti-Semitic conspiracy theories again

raised its ugly head the same year *Borat* was released, this time in the heart of Hollywood itself. On July 28, 2006, Mel Gibson was arrested for driving while intoxicated, and then proceeded to rip into the Jewish police officer who arrested him, infamously asserting that "Jews are responsible for all the wars in the world."[36] On the same day, a Muslim gunman attacked the Jewish Federation in Seattle, murdering one woman and wounding five others, a story that was tellingly overshadowed in the media by Mel Gibson's arrest.[37]

Gibson, of course, was no stranger to accusations of anti-Semitism. Even before its release, his film about the crucifixion of Jesus, *The Passion of the Christ* (2004),[38] had been roundly condemned because most of its villains were Jewish caricatures. Critics argued that the movie would rekindle the deadly canard that "the Jews killed Christ," and even inspire physical violence against Jewish victims in the same way that medieval Passion Plays had. As Peter Boyer noted in his review for *The New Yorker*, Gibson originally used a controversial line from the Gospel of Matthew, a line that only appears in that gospel; after Pilate publicly and symbolically washes his hands of Jesus, someone from the Jewish crowd cries, "His blood be on us, and our children." In response to criticism, Gibson removed the subtitle of the line, but the line was still spoken as untranslated Aramaic.[39]

Happily, very few incidents of violence were convincingly attributed to *The Passion of the Christ* after its release. Two years later, the controversy had faded. Then came Gibson's arrest, and the actor's real feelings about Jewish people were once again the object of speculation. It didn't help that Gibson's father, crypto-Catholic extremist Hutton Gibson, is a vocal Holocaust denier, prone to public pronouncements that Jews were plotting to create "one world religion and one world government" as part of a conspiracy involving the U.S. Federal Reserve and the Vatican![40]

Incredibly, *South Park* seemed to predict Gibson's post-arrest meltdown two years before it happened. A 2004 episode called "The Passion of the Jew" lampooned the controversy surrounding *The Passion of the Christ*.[41] This action-packed episode sees the boys trying to get their money back after going to see *The Passion*, thinking it would be another *Braveheart*—all except Cartman, who's inspired to start a Christian revival that will usher in a second Holocaust. In this episode, Gibson is depicted as an unhinged maniac on a rampage who refuses to refund the kids' ticket money, flinging feces and shouting in German.

Tasteless in the extreme? You bet. But maybe insane times dictate equally insane humor. Luckily, another showbiz Mel offers words of wisdom for a world gone crazy, assuring us that humor—even the over-the-top, tasteless jokes favored by our post modern jesters—is a powerful defense against an equally crazy universe. The zany writer and director behind *Blazing Saddles* and *Young Frankenstein*, Mel Brooks pioneered today's edgy humor with *The Producers* back in 1968, a movie about two Jews mounting a musical called "Springtime for Hitler."[42] Sensing that the time was ripe, Brooks revived *The Producers* on Broadway in 2001 (then filmed it again in 2005!) That "new" Broadway show became the hottest ticket on the Great White Way, while grabbing a record number of Tony Awards.

Finding himself back in the news all over again, Brooks explained his lifelong dedication to tasteless, over-the-top satire: "If you stand on a soapbox and trade rhetoric with a dictator you never win…That's what they do so well: They seduce people. But if you ridicule them, bring them down with laughter, they can't win. You show how crazy they are."[43]

CONCLUSION

COOL, JEW?

"Brisket is the part of the cow that only a Jew can find."[1]
—*Lewis Black*

In the final episode of the fifth season of *Curb Your Enthusiasm*, Larry learns that he was adopted as a child, so he *schleps* to Arizona to meet his biological parents, the Cohens.[2] Once there, Larry finds out that the Cohens are actually the Cones. "I'm Gentile!" a shocked Larry declares.

After this *shtick* shift, Larry suddenly changes from a Jewish into a Gentile stereotype. He goes to church, rides horses, fixes cars, fishes, shoots guns, does some roofing, and chugs beer. The catch is Larry wasn't really adopted; he was Jewish all along, and as soon as he finds that out, he immediately shifts back to being his old *kvetchaholic* self.

But the choice of Cohen vs. Cone is one that American Jews have faced over the last century. More and more, we're choosing "Cohen." In *Shtick Shift*, we've met a new generation of Jewish humorists who are more comfortable in their Semitic skins than their comedic ancestors, and highly adept at exploring contemporary Jewish concerns.

For much of the twentieth century, Jewish entertainers anglicized their names—or had it done for them by studio executives—to hide their heritage and become perfectly white-bread Americans. Today, the situation is completely reversed. The advent of the hipster Jew reflects the fact that Jews are increasingly outspoken about their ethnic origin and identity, and today's Jewish comedians seem poised to dominate and define another century of humor. America has been "Fockerized."

The old garment industry motto used to go: "Dress British, think Yiddish.") This became the unofficial slogan for millions of Jews, until today. In the twenty-first century, big noses are back and Jewfros and JAPs are now symbols of Jewish pride.

The infamous "Chrismukkah" celebration notwithstanding, "Christmas tree envy" is no more. We're a long way from Jewish songwriter Irving Berlin penning the most beloved paean to a Christian holiday ever, "White Christmas," not to mention "Easter Parade." Today, Jewish hipsters can be found at the many "*Matzoh* Ball" singles schmooze parties, sipping Manischewitz cocktails and singing, "I'm Dreaming of a Happy Chanukah."

In the first decade of the new century, today's younger generation identifies more with these superficial trappings of Jewish culture than with ancient traditions. Yet unlike their *bubbes* and *zadies*, these young men and women are happy to identify themselves as flamingly Jewish. They read *Heeb* magazine, the journal *Zeek*, books like *Cool Jew: The Ultimate Guide for Every Member of the Tribe* and Jewcy.com, and listen to Klezmer combos and blatantly Jewish hip-hop and indie bands like Y-Love and Pharoah's Daughter.

Jewish youth may be poking fun and laughing from the pews at the back of the synagogue, but at least they're back in. And Sunday School just got more interesting with the Judd Apatow-produced, Harold Ramis-directed *Year One* (2009), staring Jack Black. Set in biblical times, we have the Sephardic Hank Azaria playing orginal member of the tribe, Abraham.

Jewish culture is being celebrated, reinvented and reinvigorated, and innovations in comedy have been a major contributor. As we've seen, humor has always provided Jews with a safe way to explore their identities. Movies like *Meet the Fockers* offer comical takes on intermarriage and the changing face of the Jewish family, while Sarah Silverman is bent on pushing the JAP stereotype to the edge of absurdity. The ambiguity of assimilation still drives Jewish humorists crazy after all these years, as does anti-Semitism—just look at the politically incorrect dialogue in *Borat*. Having grown up with relative material security and success, young Jewish comedians are less afraid to explore the darker implications of conspicuous consumption in shows like *Entourage*. Instead of being castigated for bringing up the notion that "the Jews run Hollywood," Larry David has made a critically acclaimed show out of that once forbidden subject with *Curb Your Enthusiasm*.

Still, this renewed sense of pride and confidence also risks devaluing the faith by poking fun at Judaism without exploring its substance. Herein lies the dilemma: Now that the hipster Jew movement is a marketable brand, should we officially declare it over? Has today's riotous comedy become the new "establishment," and if so, do its millions of fans risk becoming conformists who only think they're rebels, snugly, smugly ensconced in a postmodern Borscht Belt?

With all of our sophistication, contemporary Jews still seem incapable of fully escaping the Catskills. Witness ultra-hip comic Lewis Black, still making jokes about brisket, while Jon Stewart's slick "Tribeca" intellectual humor retains the cadence of the Borscht Belt. This again begs the question "Can you take the Jew out of the *shtetl*, but not take the *shtetl* out of the Jew?" Or as in the case of Larry David's Brentwood, does it just becomes another *shtetl*?

Jews are today less afraid to highlight the things that mark them as different. By accentuating Jewish stereotypes, we also come to realize that they no longer ring completely true. Jokes about Jewish mothers aren't as funny as they used to be because they no longer reflect reality (although Larry David's postmodern *schlemiel* never seems to go out of style). When young Jewish comics quip about creaky stereotypes, it's as if they're exaggerating old-fashioned Jewish humor in an attempt to say goodbye to it once and for all. However, audiences may not be willing to let it go just yet. Jewish and Gentile audiences alike are fans of both Sacha Baron Cohen's "Jewish minstrelsy" and Larry David and Jon Stewart's yiddishisms.

Consider the spokesman for the politically savvy voter in the 2008 election, Jon Stewart.

Who could have predicted back in 1999 that the star of *The Daily Show* would become the new Walter

Cronkite? In a January 12, 2006, interview with former federal prosecutor Edward Lazarus about Judge Samuel Alito's confirmation hearing, Lazarus told Stewart that Alito was "very, very conservative." Stewart had the *chutzpah* to ask, "Um, what's going to happen to Jews? Are we, are we uh…are we going to be asked to leave, do you know? May we stay?"[3]

Actually, that's not such a bad question. The year 2006 saw the release of not one but two books that ask the timeless question: "Is it good for the Jews?" These two books with almost identical titles are both "hysterical," depending on which definition you're using.

One book, *Is It Good for the Jews?* by Stephen Schwartz (a Jewish convert to Islam), is a deadly serious critique of the American "Jewish Lobby" and its supposed influence over U.S. foreign policy.[4]

Comic relief comes in the form of *Yes, But Is It Good for the Jews?*, by (still Jewish) Jonny Geller, who asks, "How often, at the end of a long argument on Friedman economic theory or the real implications of the U.S. government's reluctance to join the Kyoto treaty on climate change, have you spoken, breathlessly, the words you knew were on everybody else's lips around that Shabbos dinner table: 'Yes, but is it good for the Jews?'"[5]

(And how can we overlook the irreverent musical duo David Fagin and Rob Tannenbaum, who call themselves Good for the Jews and whose songs—with titles like "It's Good to Be a Jew at Christmas"—make fun of bar mitzvahs, Chanukah and Mel Gibson.)[6]

So let's think again about *Borat*'s exposé of anti-Semitism. "Throw the Jew Down the Well!" is now a pop-

ular cell phone tune. Will the Borat shtick actually perpetuate the very stereotypes it purports to condemn?

In other words, is today's humor good for the Jews?

The answer is an unqualified... maybe.

If *Borat* isn't good for the Jews, that isn't the fault of
his Jewish creator. The Jewish people face many threats
in the twenty-first century and contemporary comedy
simply reflects this. Let's not shoot the messenger or
blame the victim: The real culprits these days are blood-
thirsty tyrants and relatively puny homegrown cranks.
That Jewish comics have so much material to work with
reflects a sad—even scary—reality.

But despite the anti-Semitism that persists in the
world, today's Jewish comics choose to stay Jewish in the
face of seductive assimilation. This crazy bicultural pol-
lination can only help Jewish comics rise to meet the
challenges of today. And they're doing this in perfect
sync with the times.

Ten years after his sitcom ended, Jerry Seinfeld returned with the animated film *Bee Movie*.[7] Seinfeld
voices a bee from the Upper West Side of Manhattan
named Barry Bee Benson who's at home on the *bee-mah*.
A deeper glance shows a subtext swarming with Jewish
jokes about bees being "bee-ish" (as opposed to—wait
for it—WASPs). There is even a Holocaust metaphor as
corporate beehives are described as "work camps" and
gaseous smoke is used to immobilize bees. Barry's *bubbe*
throws in the guilt about a girl Barry is interested in: "I
hope she's bee-ish!"

Today's humorists are bee-ing themselves.

But why is a rabbi writing about all this *schmutz*? Today's humor may be very Jewish but it is also very unkosher. As a campus rabbi, I have to understand that

comedy culture so I can understand the young people I work with. Unlike many of my rabbinic colleagues, I was not raised in a religious Jewish home; and being a former film student, Jewish representation in the media still fascinates me.

But like today's Jewish comedians, I'm just trying to be myself. I always integrate humor into everything I do. It is part of my personality, and my mission.

As mentioned in the preface, humor has a divine side. According to Jewish thought, humor even has healing powers. That's not just some flaky new-age notion, either. The Lubavitcher Rebbe, Rabbi Menachem M. Schneerson, taught that the difference between a frown and a smile is that when we frown, we freeze up; our blood does not flow and we stop being receptive vessels. Yet when we smile, we become loose and relaxed. It's simply a more healthy state-of-being. Humor takes us from constricted consciousness into the realm of expanded consciousness. This kind of heightened awareness is just what we need most right now.

The Talmud tells us that the great prophet Elijah appeared before the mystic Rabbi Beroka of Huza in the marketplace at Lapet. Rabbi Beroka asked him, "Is there anyone among all these people who will have a share in the world to come?" Elijah pointed out two men. Rabbi Beroka immediately ran over and quizzed these two individuals, asking, "What is your occupation?" figuring that they were scholars, rabbis or at the very least doctors. They replied, "We are Badhanim [Hebrew for "jesters"]. When we see someone who is sad, we cheer him up" (Talmud, Ta-anit 22a).

Let's face it: Today's racy, offensive punch lines probably weren't what the prophet had in mind. But in a nation where the most prescribed drugs are antidepressants, we all need a good laugh.

Most importantly, laughing in the face of fear is a powerful statement of defiance. In today's world, blighted as it is with conflicts and catastrophes, maybe comedy can help us cope both as ammunition against the bad guys and a morale booster for the rest of us.

Don't forget: Humor is the most powerful weapon of all. And you'll never have trouble getting it through airport security!

GLOSSARY

bee-mah – SEE bimah

bimah – Hebrew term for the platform in a synagogue from which the Torah scroll is read.

borscht – an eastern European soup made with beets, cabbage, potatoes, or other vegetables. Though not specifically Jewish, it has become a traditional soup in many Jewish homes.

bubbes – Yiddish term for grandmothers.

Chanukah – Jewish holiday celebrating the victory of the Maccabees over the Greek army in the 2nd Century BCE, and the miracle that occurred when oil in the re-dedicated Temple, which should only have burned for one day, lasted for eight days.

cholent - a dish usually consisting of meat, beans, barley and potatoes, served on the Sabbath but cooked the day before and simmered overnight over a low flame or crock pot. (The author recommends adding a can of Coca-Cola.)

chutzpah – Yiddish term for an attitude that combines gall, nerve, and arrogance.

goyim – transliterated from the Hebrew word which means "nation" or "people." Historically a synonym for Gentile or non-Jew, although in recent times the word is used with disparaging connotations.

Haftorah – Hebrew term for the portion of the Prophets which is read during the Jewish Sabbath service.

Kabbalah - literally defined as "receiving," this is the mystical aspect of Judaism. Used to describe the esoteric teachings of both the Torah and Rabbinic literature.

klutzy – Yiddish term for clumsy.

kosher – Hebrew term, referring to whether something is allowed to be eaten or used, according to dietary or ceremonial laws. In general, the term refers to whether something is correct or acceptable.

kvelling – Yiddish term for enjoying.

kvetch – Yiddish term for complain.

kvetchaholic – The author's term for someone who obsessively complains.

Manischewitz – a popular brand of sweet kosher wine, used for Sabbath or holiday meals, as well as certain Jewish ceremonies. Can be spread on bread if no jelly is available.

matzoh – Hebrew term for unleavened bread, one of the foods that must be prepared for a Passover seder. One of the commonly made foods cooked using matzoh meal is the matzoh ball, often added to chicken soup. Thus, the choice of the name "Matzo Ball" for the popular annual Jewish singles event.

mazel tov – Hebrew phrase that literally means "good luck" but is actually closer in meaning to "congratulations".

megillah – A traditional scroll containing text from the Bible. Megillat Esther (the scroll of Esther) is read annually in synagogue during the Purim festival. It has become a slang word for any tediously detailed or long-winded account.

mezuzah – A small piece of parchment inscribed with passages from the Bible, that is rolled up in a container and attached to the door frames of Jewish homes.

nachas – Yiddish term for the joy that comes from pride in achievement, especially from those of children.

nebbish – Yiddish term for a nerd.

oy vey – A Yiddish expression of shock. Literally "O woe!" from, "O woe is me."

Passover – Festival which celebrates the liberation of the Jewish slaves from their Egyptian rulers, popularized in such films as *The Prince of Egypt* and *The Ten Commandments.*

punim – Yiddish term for face.

Purim – Festival celebrating how the Jews of Persia were saved from annihilation during the rule of King Achashverosh in 4th Century BCE.

schep – Yiddish for "to obtain", usually put together with "nachas". To "schep nachas" is to get joy from something someone has done.

schlepping – Yiddish term for dragging, but usually refers to taking a long trip somewhere.

schmutz – Yiddish term for dirt or dirty.

seder – The annual ceremony during the first two nights of Passover, which includes retelling the story of the exodus from Egypt, and eating of a festive meal.

Shabbat – Hebrew word for the Jewish Sabbath, which begins at sundown on Friday evening and ends at sundown on Saturday evening. Also known as "Shabbos".

shiksa – Yiddish term for a female non-Jew. Has become a disparaging term.

shlemazel – Yiddish term for an unlucky loser.

schlemiel – Yiddish term for an inept misfit.

shmatteh – Yiddish term for an old piece of clothing or rag.

shmendrik – Yiddish term for a nincompoop.

shmo – Yiddish term for someone you pity.

shtetl – Yiddish term for a small Jewish town in Eastern Europe.

shtick – Yiddish term for a piece or a lump. It has become slang for a routine, particularly a comedy routine.

shul – Yiddish term for a synagogue.

simcha – Yiddish term for celebration. Also the name of the author of this book.

talit – A prayer shawl that is worn during morning services. Also known as a "tallis".

treif – Yiddish term for unkosher.

tuchas – Yiddish term for the part of one's anatomy one sits on.

tzurus – Yiddish term for trouble.

unkosher – Unsuitable for using or eating.

verklempt – Yiddish term for being on the verge of tears.

yarmulke – Yiddish term for a Jewish skullcap.

yeshiva – An institute of learning where the Jewish holy books and commentaries are learned, discussed and vigorously debated.

Yom Kippur – Also called the Day of Atonement. One of the holiest days of the Jewish calendar, marked by fasting and prayer for the atonement of sins. A popular prayer, "Kol Nidre," is recited during the Yom Kippur evening service. It has also been performed by such musicians as Al Jolson and Neil Diamond.

zaydes – Yiddish term for grandfathers.

zahl zine mit glick – Yiddish phrase meaning "It shall be with luck."

END NOTES

PREFACE: PUT ON YOUR *YARMULKE*

1   *Yippee: A Journey of Jewish Joy.* Dir. Paul Mazursky, the National Center for Jewish Film, 2006.

SOMETHING FROM NOTHING: JEWISH COMEDY IN A NEW CENTURY

1   William Novak and Moshe Waldoks, *The Big Book of Jewish Humor: 25th Anniversary Edition* (New York: HarperCollins Publishers, 1981, 2006).

2   Jeanna Smith Rakoff, "The New Super Jews," *Time Out New York*, 4–11 Dec. 2003: 13–16.

3   Steven M. Cohen and Ari Y. Kelman, *Cultural Events and Jewish Identity: Young Adult Jews in New York* (New York: The National Foundation for Jewish Culture and UJA-Federation of New York), 5 Feb. 2005,

http://www.jewishculture.org/content/pdf/CultureStudy.pdf.

4   *2000 Years with Carl Reiner & Mel Brooks* (LA: Capitol Records, 1960).

5   Lenny Bruce. *The Essential Lenny Bruce.* (New York: Ballantine Books, 1967) 40–41.

6   *Play It Again, Sam.* Dir. Herbert Ross. (USA: APJAC, 1972).

7   *Annie Hall.* Dir. Woody Allen. (USA: Rollins-Joffe, 1977).

8   *Blazing Saddles.* Dir. Mel Brooks. (USA: Crossbow Productions, 1974).

9   *Young Frankenstein.* Dir. Mel Brooks. (USA: Gruskoff/Venture, 1974).

10 Vincent Brooks. *Something Ain't Kosher Here: The Rise of the "Jewish" Sitcom* (New Brunswick, NJ: Rutgers University Press, 2003).

11 "The Yada Yada," *Seinfeld*, NBC, 24 Apr. 1997.

12 Phil Rosenthal, "About Larry," *The Chicago-Sun Times*, 13 Oct. 2000: 51.

13 List of *Curb Your Enthusiasm* Guest Stars, http://en.wikipedia.org/List_of_celebrities_appearing_on_Curb_Your_Enthusiasm.

14 Neal Gabler, *An Empire of Their Own: How the Jews Invented Hollywood* (New York: Doubleday, 1988), 2–4.

15 Gabler 7.

16 *Crossfire.* Dir. Edward Dmytryk. (USA: RKO Radio Pictures, 1947).

17 *Gentleman's Agreement.* Dir. Elia Kazan. (USA: Twentieth Century-Fox, 1947).

18 David Zurawik, *The Jews of Prime Time* (Lebanon, NH: Brandeis University Press, 2003), 8.

19 Zurawik, 58.

20 *For Your Consideration.* Dir. Christopher Guest, perf. Harry Shearer, Catherine O'Hara, Michael McKean, and Ricky Gervais (USA: Warner Independent Pictures, 2006).

21 *Eight Crazy Nights.* Dir. Seth Kearsley, perf. Adam Sandler, Rob Schneider, and Jon Lovitz, (USA: Columbia Pictures, 2002).

22 Abigail Pogrebin, *Stars of David: Prominent Jews Talk About Being Jewish* (New York: Random House-Broadway Books, 2005), 9–17.

JEW GOLD: SELF-FULFILLING STEREOTYPES AND UN-FULFILLING WEALTH

1 "Two Days Before the Day After Tomorrow," *South Park*, Comedy Central, 19 Oct. 2005.

2 Edna Bonocich, "A Theory of Middleman Minorities," *American Sociological Review* 38 (1973): 583.

3 Thomas Sowell, *Black Rednecks and White Liberals* (San Francisco: Encounter Books, 2005), 72.

4 Simon Louvish, *Monkey Business: The Lives and Legends of the Marx Brothers* (New York: St. Martin's Press, 1999), 8.

5 "Return of the King," *Entourage*, HBO, 6 May 2007.

6   See the chapter Seriously Funny.

7   *Heeb,* Spring 2006.

8   Sanford Pinsker, "Staying at the Head of the (Humor) Class: Can Jewish-American Humor Survive the Assimilationist 21st Century?" *MyJewishLearning.com,* http://www.myjewishlearning.com/culture/Humor/HumorHistory/JHumorAmerica/21stCentJHumor.htm.

9   Saul Bellow.

10 "The 5 Wood," *Curb Your Enthusiasm,* HBO, 1 Feb. 2004.

11 Sigmund Freud, *Jokes and Their Relation to the Unconscious* (New York: W. W. Norton & Co., Inc, 1905), 133.

12 "Shaq," *Curb Your Enthusiasm,* HBO, 11 Nov. 2001.

13 Maurice Friedman. *A Dialogue with Hasidic Tales.* (NY: Human Science Press, 1988), 49–50.

14 Rabbi Joseph Telushkin, *Jewish Humor: What the Best Jewish Jokes Say About the Jews* (New York: William Morrow and Company, Inc., 1992), 73.

15 Jacob B. Ukeles and David A. Grossman, *Report on Jewish Poverty: January 2004* (New York: Metropolitan Council on Jewish Poverty and UJA-Federation of New York, 2004).

16 Special Report, "The 50 Most Generous Philanthropists," *Business Week,* 27 Nov. 2006, 75.

17 "The Anonymous Donor," *Curb Your Enthusiasm,* HBO, 16 Sep. 2007.

[18] The stereotype of the Jewish financial genius is a well-traveled one. For example, "how to" business guides capitalizing on this persistent myth are big sellers in (get this) communist China. According to the *Washington Post*, titles such as *The Legend of Jewish Wealth* and *Jewish People and Business: The Bible of How to Live Their Lives* are flying off the shelves in a nation where Jews number less than 10,000 in a nation of 1.3 billion. Wang Zhen, a researcher at the Center for Jewish Studies, told the *Post* that he recognizes that the stereotypes can be considered anti-Semitic but thinks it's important that "even if people in China have the wrong impressions of Jewish people, the Chinese are very kind to them." (Ariana Eunjung Cha, "Sold on a Stereotype," *The Washington Post,* 7 Feb. 2007: D01.)

[19] "When You Wish Upon a Weinstein," *Family Guy,* FOX, 9 Nov. 2003. FOX wouldn't originally air the episode, but it later appeared on The Cartoon Network's *Adult Swim.* FOX finally aired the episode on December 10, 2004.

[20] Optimus Prime must be Sephardic—note the Latin name.

RAISING THE BAR: BLING MITZVAH

[1] *Keeping Up with the Steins,* dir. Scott Marshall, perf. Richard Benjamin, Gary Marshall, Daryl Hannah, Larry Miller, Jeremy Piven, and Daryl Sabara (USA: Miramax, 2006).

[2] For a discussion of Jeremy Piven's portrayal of Ari Gold on HBO's *Entourage,* see the chapter "Jew

Gold: Self-Fulfilling Stereotypes and Unfulfilling Wealth."

3 Ryan Gardner Jr., "Bash Mitzvahs!" cover story, *New York Magazine*, 9 March 1998.

4 Ari L. Goldman, *Being Jewish: The Spiritual and Cultural Practice of Judaism Today*. (New York: Simon & Schuster, 2007), 66.

5 Jill Rappaport, *Mazel Tov: Celebrities' Bar and Bat Mitzvah Memories* (New York: Simon & Schuster, 2007).

6 Always a popular locale in Jewish comedy. Just think of Groucho Marx's famous one-liner/Zen koan: he wouldn't want to belong to any club that would have him as a member.

7 Lloyd Grove with Hudson Morgan, "Not-So-Petty Cash to Rock Bat Mitzvah," New York *Daily News*, 29 Nov. 2005: 32.

8 *Starsky & Hutch*. Dir. Todd Phillips (USA: Dimension Films, 2004).

9 Roger Bennett, Jules Shell, and Nick Kroll, *Bar Mitzvah Disco* (New York: Random House, Inc., 2005), 91.

10 Gardner, "Bash Mitzvahs!"

11 Julian Roman, "An Interview with the Cast of *Keeping Up with the Steins*," 12 May 2006, http://www.movieweb.com/news/49/12649.php.

12 Elizabeth Bernstein, "You Don't Have to Be Jewish to Want a Bar Mitzvah," *The Wall Street Journal*, 14 Jan. 2004: A1.

13 Carli Teproff, "A Poodle Comes of Age," *The Miami Herald*, 11 Oct. 2005: 1B.

14 Rabbis of Boca Raton Theological Society, Barbara Davilman and Ellis Weiner, *How to Raise a Jewish Dog* (New York: Little, Brown and Company, 2007).

15 Henny Youngman. *"Take My Life, Please!"* (NY: Wm. Morrow, 1991), 206.

16 "Today I Am a Clown," *The Simpsons*, FOX, 7 Dec. 2003.

17 "Like Father, Like Clown," *The Simpsons*, FOX, 24 Oct. 1991.

18 Edward S. Shapiro, *We are Many: Reflections on American Jewish History and Identity* (New York: Syracuse University Press, 2005).

19 Lisa A. Keister, "Religion and Wealth: The Role of Religious Affiliation and Participation in Early Adult Asset Accumulation," *Social Forces* 82.1, Sept. 2003: 175–207. The National Longitudinal Survey of Youth study was sponsored by the Bureau of Labor and Statistics. The 1979 study tracked over 12,000 individuals who were between the ages of fourteen and twenty-two in that year, and surveyed participants until 1998.

20 For more on the relationship between Jewish comedy and money, see the chapter "Jew Gold: Self-Fulfiling Stereotypes and UnFulfilling Wealth."

21 David Mamet, *The Wicked Son* (New York: Schocken Books, 2006), 67.

22 *The Jazz Singer.* Dir. Alan Crosland, perf. Al Jolson, May McAvoy, and Warner Oland (USA: Warner

Bros., 1927).

23 *The Jazz Singer.* Dirs. Richard Fleischer and Sidney J. Furie, perf. Neil Diamond, Laurence Olivier, and Lucie Arnaz, (USA: Associated Film Distribution, 1980).

24 Gerri Miller, "My Big Fat Jewish Bar Mitzvah" *American Jewish Life Magazine,* May/June 2006.

25 Roman, "An Interview with the Cast of *Keeping Up with the Steins.*"

26 Bradford Weiss, "Lights, Camera, Bar Mitzvah: The 'Spy Kids' Turn 13," *West Coast Chabad Lubavitch,* 7 July 2005, http://tiny.cc/HgoLd.

BEYOND BUBBE: THE 21ST CENTURY JEWISH FAMILY

1 Joel Stein, "Why Hot, WASPy Chicks Love Jews," *Los Angeles Times,* 9 Jan. 2005: M6.

2 *Meet the Fockers.* Dir. Jay Roach, perf. Ben Stiller, Robert De Niro, Dustin Hoffman, Barbra Streisand, and Teri Polo (USA: Universal Studios, 2004).

3 *Abie's Irish Rose.* Dir. Victor Fleming (USA: Paramount, 1928).

4 *Bridget Loves Bernie,* CBS, 1972–1973.

5 *Mad About You,* NBC, 1992–1999.

6 *Keeping the Faith.* Dir. Ed Norton, perf. Ben Stiller, Ed Norton, Jenna Elfman, and Anne Bancroft (USA: Touchstone Pictures, 2000).

7 *Along Came Polly.* Dir. John Hamburg, perf. Ben Stiller, Jennifer Anniston, and Philip Seymour Hoff-

man (USA: Universal Pictures, 2004.)

8   *The Heartbreak Kid.* Dir. Elaine May (USA: Palomar, 1972).

9   *The Heartbreak Kid.* Dir. Bobby Farelly and Peter Farelly (USA: Dreamworks, 2007).

10   *Knocked Up,* dir. Judd Apatow, perf. Seth Rogen, Katherine Heigl, and Paul Rudd (USA: Universal Studios, 2007).

11   *Juno.* Dir. Jason Reitman (USA: Fox Searchlight, 2007).

12   *Will & Grace,* NBC, 1998–2006.

13   Jonathan Sacks, "Studies in Renewal 2: The Crisis of Continuity," June 1993, http://www.chiefrabbi. org/articles/renewal/renewal2.html.

14   Anthony Weiss, "Study Finds Intermarriage Peak in Maine." *The Forward,* 5 Dec. 2007, http://www. forward.com/articles/12196.

15   "The Seder," *Curb Your Enthusiasm,* HBO, 13 Nov. 2005.

16   "The Pants Tent," *Curb Your Enthusiasm,* HBO, 15 Oct. 2000.

17   "The TiVo Guy," *Curb Your Enthusiasm,* HBO, 21 Oct. 2007.

18   Vincent Brook. *You Should See Yourself: Jewish Identity in Postmodern American Culture.* (New Brunswick, NJ: Rutgers University Press, 2006), 283.

19   "Mary, Joseph and Larry," *Curb Your Enthusiasm,* HBO, 10 Nov. 2002.

[20] "The Christ Nail," *Curb Your Enthusiasm,* 9 Oct. 2005.

[21] Laruie Rozakis, *The Portable Jewish Mother: Guilt, Food, and...When Are You Giving Me Grandchildren?* (Cincinnati, OH: Adams Media Corporation, 2007).

[22] Joyce Antler, *You Never Call! You Never Write!: A History of the Jewish Mother* (Oxford, UK: Oxford University Press, 2007).

[23] Marnie Winston-Macauley, *Yiddishe Mammas: The Truth About the Jewish Mother* (Kansas City, MO: Andrews McMeel Publishing, LLC, 2007).

[24] Judy Gold, *25 Questions for a Jewish Mother* (New York: Hyperion Press, 2007).

[25] *The Rise of the Goldbergs,* NBC Radio, 1929–1936; *The Goldbergs,* CBS Radio, 1936–1946; CBS Television, 1949–1951; NBC, 1952–1953; DuMont, 1954–1955.

[26] Winston-Macauley, 23.

[27] Ibid.

[28] Philip Roth, *Portnoy's Complaint* (New York: Random House-Vintage Books, 1969) 111.

[29] "Coffee Talk," *Saturday Night Live,* NBC, 1991–1994.

[30] *The Nanny,* CBS, 1993–1999.

[31] "Mr. Hankey's Christmas Classic," *South Park,* Comedy Central, 1 Dec. 1999.

[32] *The Hebrew Hammer.* Dir. Jonathan Kesselman, perf. Adam Goldberg, Judy Greer, Andy Dick, and Mario Van Peebles (USA: Comedy Central Films, 2003).

[33] *Moonstruck.* Dir. Norman Jewison, perf. Cher, Nicholas Cage, and Olympia Dukakis (USA: MGM, 1987).

[34] *My Big Fat Greek Wedding.* Dir. Joel Zwick, perf. Nia Vardalos, John Corbett, Lainie Kazan, and Michael Constantine, Warner Bros., 2002.

[35] *Everybody Loves Raymond,* CBS, 1996–2005.

[36] Antler, 236.

[37] Another word frequently used to describe the JAP is "cold."

[38] Herman Wouk, *Marjorie Morningstar* (New York: Back Bay Books, 1955).

[39] As described in Evelyn Torton Beck. "From 'Kike' to 'JAP'" *Sojourner: The Women's Forum* (1988): 18–23.

[40] Philip Roth, *Goodbye, Columbus* (Boston: Houghton Mifflin Company, 1959).

[41] Gail Parent, *Sheila Levine Is Dead and Living in New York* (New York: Overlook TP, 1972).

[42] Gilda Radner, "Jewess Jeans," *Saturday Night Live,* NBC, 16 Feb. 1979.

[43] *Private Benjamin.* Dir. Howard Zieff (USA: Warner Bros., 1980).

[44] *Clueless.* Dir. Amy Heckerling, perf. Alicia Silverstone, Stacey Dash, Brittany Murphy, and Dan Hedaya (USA: Paramount Pictures, 1995).

[45] Isabel Rose. *The J.A.P. Chronicles.* (NY: Broadway Books, 2006).

[46] Alan Newhouse, "The Return of the JAP," *The Boston Globe,* March 13, 2005: D4.

47   Troy Patterson, "Queen of Farts: Lost in the Shallows of the Sarah Silverman Program," *Slate.com*, Feb. 1, 2007.

48   Ruthe Stein, "Sarah Silverman—Soo Not PC, So Very Funny," *The San Francisco Chronicle*, Nov. 18, 2005: E5.

49   Quoted in Patterson, "Queen of Farts: Lost in the Shallows of the Sarah Silverman Program"

50   *Annie Hall.* Dir. Woody Allen, perf. Woody Allen, Diane Keaton, Tony Roberts, and Christopher Walken (USA: United Artists, 1977).

51   Bryan Fogel and Sam Wolfson, *Jewtopia*, dirs. Andy Fickman and John Tillinger, 2003–2007.

52   *The Apprenticeship of Duddy Kravitz.* Dir. Ted Kotcheff. Canada: Astral Bellevue Pathe, 1974.

53   *Jaws.* Dir. Steven Spielberg (USA: Zanuck / Brown, 1975).

54   *The Goodbye Girl.* Dir. Herbert Ross (USA: MGM, 1977).

55   *The 40-Year-Old Virgin.* Dir. Judd Apatow (USA: Universal, 2005).

56   *Knocked Up.* Dir. Judd Apatow (USA: Universal, 2007).

57   *Superbad.* Dir. Greg Mottola (USA: Columbia, 2007).

58   *Hot Rod.* Dir. Akiva Schaffer (USA: Paramount, 2007).

59   *You Don't Mess with the Zohan.* Dir. Dennis Dugan. (USA: Sony, 2008).

60 *Arrested Development,* FOX, 2003–2006.

61 "The Chrismukk-huh?" *The O.C.,* FOX, 14 Dec. 2006.

62 "The Year in Buzzwords" *Time* 30 Dec. 2004, http://www.time.com/time/magazine/ article/0,9171,1009917,00.html.

63 Also see the book by Ron Gompertz. *Chrismukkah: Everything You Need to Know to Celebrate the Hybrid Holiday* (NY: Stewart, Tabori & Chang, 2006) and the companion Web site http://www.chrismukkah. com.

FAKE NEWS, REAL IMPACT

1 *The Daily Show with Jon Stewart,* Comedy Central, 10 April 2007.

2 *That Was the Week That Was,* BBC, 1962–1963.

3 Not the Nine O'Clock News, BBC, 1978–1982.

4 The 57th Annual Primetime Emmy Awards, CBS, 18 Sept. 2005.

5 The Pew Center for the People & the Press, *News Audiences Increasingly Politicized.* (Washington, D.C.: The Pew Research Center, 8 June 2004).

6 The Pew Center for the People & the Press, *Public Knowledge of Current Affairs Changed Little by News and Information Revolutions.*(Washington, D.C.: The Pew Research Center, 15 April 2007).

7 Producer (and Jewish comic writer) Judd Apatow played with this in *Anchorman: The Legend of Ron*

Burgundy (USA: Dreamworks, 2004). The water-skiing squirrel in the beginning of the film was real news footage.

8   Think of Mel Brooks' character Comicus from the 1981 film *History of the World, Part* I—a stand-up philosopher.

9   The Web site Technorati attempts to aggregate the blogosphere, and founder Dave Sifry offers quarterly State of the Blogosphere updates, which track the numbers <http://www.technorati.com>. However, the numbers are certainly greater; Technorati only began including social networking sites with blog components in 2006, it doesn't track private, in-house corporate blogs that opt-out of Technorati, and 2007 saw the advent of new, fast, microblogging technology with Twitter, Jaiku, Tumblelog, and Pownce.

10   Jon Stewart and the writers of *The Daily Show, America (the Book): A Citizen's Guide to Democracy Inaction* (New York: Warner Books, 2004).

11   *Crossfire*, CNN, 15 Oct. 2004.

12   Daniel Kurtzman. "Jon Stewart's Wish Fulfilled; 'Crossfire' to Stop 'Hurting America.'" 7 Jan. 2005, http://politicalhumor.about.com/b/2005/01/07/jon-stewarts-wish-fulfilled-crossfire-to-stop-hurting-america.htm.

13   Ibid.

14   You're on Notice: "Truthiness" Picked as Word of the Year," Associated Press, 9 Dec. 2006.

15   *The Colbert Report*, Comedy Central, 26 Sept. 2006.

(You can really call the number.)

16 *The Daily Show*, Comedy Central, 2 Nov. 2006.

17 Richard Rabkin, "The Daily Show with Rob Kutner: An Interview with the Four-Time Emmy Award Winning Comedy Writer," *Jewlarious.com*, 14 Jan. 2007, http://www.aish.com/jewlariousFeatures/ jewlariousFeaturesDefault/The_Daily_Show_with_ Rob_Kutner.asp.

18 Mort Sahl, *Heartland* (New York: Harcourt Brace Jovanovich, 1976), 87.

19 John Rogers, "Mort Sahl, Once Comedy's 'Angry Young Man,' Looks at Life at 80," *The Associated Press*, 26 June 2007.

20 Lewis Black, *Comedy Central Presents: Lewis Black*, Comedy Central, 22 April 2002.

21 Lawrence Jeffrey Epstein, *The Haunted Smile: The Story of Jewish Comedians in America.* (New York: Public Affairs, 2002), 231.

22 Lewis Black, *Red, White & Screwed*, HBO, 10 June 2004.

23 William Novak and Moshe Waldoks, *The Big Book of Jewish Humor* (New York: HarperPerennial, 1981), 51.

24 Jerry Bock, Joseph Stein and Sheldon Harnick. *Fiddler on the Roof.* (Pocket Books, 1964), 8.

25 *The Daily Show*, Comedy Central, 20 Sept. 2001.

26 *Looking for Comedy in the Muslim World.* Dir. Albert Brooks, perf. Albert Brooks, Sheetal Sheth, Jon Tenney, John Carroll Lynch, Fred Thompson, War-

ner Independent Pictures, 2006.

[27] It was far different from the hugely successful *Borat*, which despite its colossal daring, seemed to suggest that world Jewry had more to fear from rednecks than from the only group that escaped Sacha Baron Cohen's satirical laser beam: radical Muslim terrorists.

[28] *Man of the Year.* Dir. Barry Levinson, perf. Robin Williams, Christopher Walken, Lewis Black, Laura Linney, Jeff Goldblum (USA: Universal Pictures, 2006).

SERIOUSLY FUNNY: ANTI-SEMITISM AND SELF-HATRED

[1] "The Four Gospels of Mel: James Mee, Ari Emanuel, Alan Nierob, Kevin Youkilis," *The Forward,* 10 Nov. 2006, http://www.forward.com/articles/8352.

[2] Michael Elkin, "Boo Borat or Praise Him?" *Jewish Exponent,* 2 Nov. 2006, http://www.jewishexponent.com/article/11139.

[3] The song is also the eighth track of the CD *Stereophonic Musical Leanings that Have Been Origin in Moving Film "Borat: Cultural Learnings of America for Make Benefit Glorious Nation of Kazakhstan"* (Atlantic Records, 2006).

[4] *Borat: Cultural Learnings of America for Make Benefit Glorious Nation of Kazakhstan.* Dir. Larry Charles. (USA: Dune Entertainment, 2006).

[5] Laura Bly, "Finding the Real Kazakhstan," *USA Today,* 16 Nov. 2006.

6   Erlan Idrissov, "We survived Stalin and we can certainly overcome Borat's slurs," *The Times* (London), 4 Nov. 2006: 25.

7   Report on Global Anti-Semitism (Washington, DC: U.S. Department of State, 2004).

8   "Iran Leader Urges Destruction of 'Cancerous' Israel," CNN.com, Reuters, 15 Dec. 2000, http://archives.cnn.com/2000/WORLD/meast/12/15/mideast.iran.reut/.

9   *A Rider Without a Horse*, [Egypt], 2002–2003.

10 Philip Graves, "Jewish World Plot—An Exposure: The Truth At Last," *The Times* (London), 16 Aug. 1921: 9.

11 Gabriel Schoenfeld, *The Return of Anti-Semitism.* (San Francisco: Encounter Books, 2004),

12 "Police Find Swastika Cut Into Acres of N.J. Cornfield," 24 Sep. 2007, http://www.nbc10.com/news/14193066/detail.html.

13 Phil Couvrette, "Jews Facing 'Gathering Storm,' Cotler Tells Israeli Audience," *The Gazette* (Montreal), 11 July 2007: A4.

14 "British Delight Over Globe Nods," BBC News, 15 Dec. 2006, http://news.bbc.co.uk/2/hi/entertainment/6182035.stm.

15 Neil Strauss, "The Man Behind the Mustache," *Rolling Stone*, 30 Nov. 2006: 56–58, 62, 64, 68, 70.

16 Sharon Waxman, "Equal-Opportunity Offender Plays Anti-Semitism for Laughs," *The New York Times*, 7 Sept. 2006: E1.

17 Dan Williams, "Could Borat's Anti-Semitism Be Good For the Jews?" *Reuters*, 6 Nov. 2006, http://www.reuters.com/article/worldNews/idUSL0639578320061106.

18 *Life Is Beautiful.* Dir. Roberto Benigni. (Italy: Cecchi Gori Group Tiger Cinematografica, 1998).

19 Art Spiegelman. *Maus: A Survivor's Tale.* (NY: Pantheon, 1991).

20 Sam Gross. *We Have Ways of Making You Laugh: 120 Funny Swastika Cartoons* (NY: Simon & Schuster, 2008).

21 Annette Insdorf. *Indelible Shadows: Film and the Holocaust* (New York: Cambridge UP, 1989, 2003).

22 "The Raincoats," *Seinfeld*, NBC, 28 Apr. 1994.

23 "The Survivor," *Curb Your Enthusiasm*, HBO, 7 March 2004.

24 *Sarah Silverman: Jesus Is Magic.* Dir. Liam Lynch, perf. Sarah Silverman, Laura Silverman, Brian Posehn, and Bob Odenkirk (USA: Black Gold Films, 2005).

25 Jimmy Kimmel, Director Bobcat Goldthwaite, ABC, 10 Nov. 2003.

26 "The Survivor," *Curb Your Enthusiasm*.

27 "The Terrorist Attack," *Curb Your Enthusiasm*, HBO, 13 Oct. 2002.

28 Konnelyn Feig, *Hitler's Death Camps: The Sanity of Madness.* (New York: Holmes & Meier, 1979), 77.

29 "Trick or Treat," *Curb Your Enthusiasm*, HBO, 7 Oct. 2001.

[30] Woody Allen, "Random Reflections of a Second-Rate Mind," *The Best American Essays 1991*, ed. Joyce Carol Oates. (New York: Ticknor and Fields, 1991), 5.

[31] "Today I Am a Clown," *The Simpsons*, FOX, 7 Dec. 2003.

[32] Jonathan Leggett, "G2: Shortcuts: Anti-Semitism, the Jewish Way," *The Guardian*, 3 March 2006: Features 2.

[33] Jonathan Leggett, "Anti-Semitism, the Jewish Way," *The Guardian*, 2006 Mar. 3, http://www.guardian.co.uk/theguardian/2006/mar/03/features11.g2.

[34] "Analyzing Jewish Comics," *Time*, 2 Oct. 1978, 235.

[35] David Deutsch and Joshua Newman. *Big Book of Jewish Conspiracies* (NY: St. Martin's Griffin, 2005).

[36] "The Four Gospels of Mel: James Mee, Ari Emanuel, Alan Nierob, Kevin Youkilis," *The Forward*, 10 Nov. 2006, http://www.forward.com/articles/8352.

[37] Carol Smith, Phuong Cat Le and Amy Rolph, "Gunman Shoots 6 at Jewish Charity, 1 Woman Dead, 5 Injured in Belltown," *Seattle Post-Intelligencer*, 29 July 2006: A1.

[38] *The Passion of the Christ*. Dir. Mel Gibson. USA: Icon Productions, 2004.

[39] Peter J. Boyer, "The Jesus War: Mel Gibson's Obsession," *The New Yorker*, 15 Sept. 2003: 58.

[40] "Gibson's Dad Calls Holocaust Mostly Fiction; Son Mel Facing Heat Over Christ Film," *The Houston Chronicle*, 20 Feb. 2004: A2.

[41] "The Passion of the Jew," *South Park*, Comedy Cen-

tral, 31 March 2004.

42   *The Producers.* Dir. Mel Brooks (USA: Crossbow Productions, 1968).

43   Nancy Shute, "20 Mel Brooks," *U.S. News & World Report,* 20 Aug. 2001: 71.

CONCLUSION: COOL JEW?

1   Lewis Black. *Heros of Jewish Comedy.* Dir. Lisa Charles and Tina Jenkins. Channel 4 Television Corporation, 2003.

2   "The End," *Curb Your Enthusiasm,* HBO, 4 Dec. 2005.

3   *The Daily Show,* Comedy Central, 12 Jan. 2006.

4   Stephen Schwartz. *Is It Good for the Jews?: The Crisis of America's Israel Lobby* (New York: Doubleday, 2006).

5   Jonny Geller. *Yes, But Is It Good for the Jews?: A Beginner's Guide,* Volume 1. (New York: Bloomsbury, 2006) introduction.

6   See their Web site http://www.goodforthejews.net.

7   *Bee Movie.* Dir. Steve Hickner and Simon J. Smith (USA: Dreamworks Animation, 2007).